D1765989

UCK

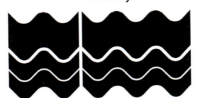

East Sussex
County Council

Not for
Loan

SUSSEX A   :RVICES

04617711 - **ITEM**

First Edition

Published in 2020 by

Woodfield Publishing Ltd
www.woodfieldpublishing.co.uk

Copyright © 2020 Brian Janman

All rights reserved

The right of Brian Janman to be identified as author of this work has been asserted in accordance with the Copyright, Designs and Patents Act 1988

Apart from any use permitted under UK copyright law, this publication may not be reproduced, stored, or transmitted, in any form, or by any means, without prior permission in writing from the Publisher.

Every effort has been made to fulfil requirements with regard to the reproduction of copyright material. The author and publisher will rectify any deficiency at the earliest opportunity if duly notified.

The opinions expressed in this book are entirely the author's own and do not represent those of Woodfield Publishing Limited or its directors.

The factual accuracy of statements made in this book is not guaranteed and the Publisher accepts no liability for any inaccuracies or omissions.

ISBN 1-84683-194-2

Printed & bound in England

Typesetting & page design: Nico Pastorius
Cover design: Klaus Schaffer

Source document
Sussex Ambulance and First Aid Services (final).ppp

Sussex Ambulance & First Aid Services

An Illustrated History

Brian Janman

woodfieldpublishing.co.uk

Publishing Ltd

WOODFIELD

independent book publishers

Woodfield Publishing Ltd

Bognor Regis ~ West Sussex ~ England ~ PO21 5EL

tel 01243 821234 ~ **e/m** info@woodfieldpublishing.co.uk

Interesting and informative books on a variety of subjects

For full details of all our published titles, visit our website at
www.woodfieldpublishing.co.uk

This book is dedicated to all those men and women, past and present, who have manned the first aid posts and crewed the ambulances in Sussex and elsewhere.

They were, and still are, a special breed of person, and we all owe them an immense debt of gratitude.

The Brougham style (above) and the Bus style
(below) are examples of the kind of horse
drawn ambulance that would have been in use
throughout Sussex at the turn of the century.

CONTENTS

About the Author

Brian Janman joined the West Sussex Ambulance Service in 1975 and qualified as a Paramedic in 1993. His service career came to an end in 1998 when he retired injured from Sussex Ambulance Service but, after recovery, he resumed his career as an independent paramedic working mainly in motor sport, with a little bit of TV work thrown in, including four years as part of the safety team covering the BBC's *Top Gear* programme. He is also a member of both the East and West Sussex Ambulance Service Retirement Associations and continues to research and record the history and development of the first aid and ambulance services in his home county of Sussex.

Foreword

THIS IS THE SECOND BOOK on the history of the Ambulance service in Sussex to be written by Brian and it is testament to the hours of research that he has undertaken over the years to amass both the information and photographic records which together combine to record the development of the ambulance service in Sussex. It is admirable that all this is recorded and kept for future generations as in my experience much of our history and heritage has been lost or consigned to the rubbish bin. The ambulance service is an integral part of our social history in terms of the modern society in which we now live and as such deserves to be properly recorded.

The ambulance service in terms of being a uniformly organised and delivered free service began on 5th July, 1948 as a result of the 1946 National Health Service Act. It has been in a continual state of development and improvement since then as it attempts to meet the ever increasing demand s made upon it. Prior to this time ambulance s were provided by various means and organisations. This volume traces a number of those developments locally as the service has evolved.

The photos and information contained within this book will take the reader through the changes that have taken place. Whether you are a serious student of ambulance service development or enjoy immersing yourself in nostalgia this volume will adequately satisfy your interest. This volume places on record details of a service that has changed over the years and seeks to develop and evolve in the future to meet the healthcare needs of our patients.

It is always mindful to remember the early pioneers of the ambulance service, when origins are traced back to the end of the 19th and through the 20th centuries, and recognise the contribution they made. The staff then, who were often referred to as "ambulance drivers" nevertheless upheld the true vocation of the service. "For the Service of Mankind" has been one of the underpinning principles of the ambulance service. These pioneers did indeed serve their patients and in doing so laid the foundations for the modern service we see today and as such we do indeed owe them a debt of gratitude.

My thanks to Brian for all his hard work and I hope you enjoy reading this book.

Andrew Parr, MSc., CertEd*

---

* Andy Parr first joined the Hastings Ambulance Service in 1968, having previously been a member of the Hastings Division of the St. John Ambulance Brigade. He went on to have a long and successful career serving in the Hastings, East Sussex, Sussex and South East Coast Ambulance Services in turn, and his knowledge of the ambulance services of East Sussex has been invaluable in the preparation of this book.

APPEAL FOR £1,000,000.

British ✝ Farmers'
Red Cross Fund.

Great Gift Sale

On behalf of the above Fund, will be held at the

Old West Street Brewery,
WORTHING ROAD, HORSHAM, on

Thursday, 1st February, 1917.

PRESIDENT—SIR MERRIK RAYMOND BURRELL.

THE SALE WILL COMMENCE AT 11 a.m.

PRESENT ENTRIES include:—1 TON OF SUGAR, in 12lb. bags; Fat Beasts; well-bred young Horses; Calves, Rams, Fat Pigs, and Goats; 2 Dogs; a quantity of Live Poultry; 2 valuable Sittings Eggs; Vehicles, Implements; Corn, Hay and Roots; and Miscellaneous Articles: including a Piano, Pathescope, valuable Old Shakespeare Prints, a Mandarin Cloak, Carved Screen, Old Silver and Copper Coins, Old Cut Glass, etc., etc. Catalogues 1d. each (free to subscribers).

Hon. Auctioneers: Messrs. Bannister & Co., Churchman & Sons, Gilbert Gardner, and King & Chasemore.

A Committee of Ladies will provide LUNCHEONS & TEAS; the former at 2s. and 1s.; latter 9d.

BAND volunteered by members of Horsham Town and Recreation Bands. Entrance 6d. until 2 p.m., after 3d.

THE WHOLE OF THE PROCEEDS will be handed over to the BRITISH FARMERS' RED CROSS FUND.

Will You Come?

200b

THE

BRITISH RED CROSS

(Men's Detachment Sussex 47)

in conjunction with

ST. JOHN AMBULANCE BRIGADE

(Bognor Regis Division)

are holding a

CHARITY BALL

on

FRIDAY, JANUARY 19th

From 9 p.m. — 2 a.m.

They will present

VICTOR SYLVESTER

and his famous

★ B.B.C. BALLROOM ORCHESTRA ★

also a

★ STAR CABARET ★

at the

PAVILION, BOGNOR REGIS

TICKETS 7/6 EACH

To be obtained from: Dr. A. R. GRAY, St. Albans, Clarence Road, Bognor Regis. Telephone 27.
NEVILLE HADCOCK, Esq., Sudley Lodge, Bognor Regis. Telephone 458.
or at THE PAVILION BOX OFFICE. Telephone 212.

FREE CAR PARK. ● FULLY LICENSED

Introduction

The British Red Cross Society was founded in 1870, soon after the outbreak of the Franco-Prussian War. Initially known as the National Society for Aid to the Sick and Wounded in War, and adopting the now famous Red Cross on a white background as its badge, the movement spread quickly across the country, and was renamed as the British Red Cross Society in 1905, the Sussex Branch being formed the same year.

The society sent surgeons, nurses and medical supplies abroad to various wars, setting up field hospitals and assisting with the repatriation and rehabilitation of the wounded. During the First World War it worked in conjunction with the Order of St. John, recruiting and training the Voluntary Aid Detachments used to reinforce the army's own medical services.

Some Sussex branches of the society operated their own ambulances or provided the volunteers to crew vehicles operated by other organisations. In 1934 for example a report states that ambulances operated or manned by the Society covered a total of 26,022 miles and conveyed 1,431 patients.

The British Order of St. John of Jerusalem founded the St. John Ambulance Association on July 1st 1877 with the aim of instructing people in first aid to the Injured and the distribution of ambulance equipment, and within a short period of time centres had been established across the country, including some in factories, collieries and railway companies.

Funds to support the work were raised by public donations and annual subscriptions. 'Corps' of volunteers who had been taught first aid by the Association were formed, the first in London, and on St. John's Day in 1887 the St. John Ambulance Brigade was instituted as 'a voluntary civilian organisation for rendering assistance in cases of accident or sudden illness in civilian emergencies', and became the uniformed branch of the Order as we know it today

One of the earliest of the St. John Ambulance Association centres in Sussex was formed in Bognor in 1885. In the same year the centre opened a subscription to purchase an 'Ambulance Van', and the centre's annual report of 1887 states 'That one has now been purchased, along with one horse to pull it, and that it will be housed by the Bognor Urban District Council.'

References

Ambulances...Chris Batten, 1996

Ambulance Handbook 6th edition...George Thomas Beaton, 1898

Autographs from a VAD Nurse: Filsham Park Hospital.................................Celia McLaren

Brighton Ambulance Service, 1946-1974...James Type

Brighton Division...David Shelton

First Aid to the Sick & Injured 17th Edition................................Warwick & Tunstall,1939

NHS Ambulances, The First 25 years..Chris Batten, 1998

Now Another Pharaoh..P.R. Thatcher, 1988

St. John Ambulance Crawley Division 1928-52, A Short History....................Simon Redhead

St. John Ambulance Littlehampton, A Short History.................................W.R. Kemp

St. John Ambulance Horsham Division 1906 - 1926 - 1976, A History...........Frank Holmes

St. John in Focus.......................Museum of the Order of St. John of Jerusalem, London, 1987

The Ambulance...Katherine Traver Barrkley, 1990

The Health of the County annual reports..............West Sussex County Council, 1961-1972

The Red Cross Then and Now...Richard Cavendish, 1984

Acknowledgements

The list of individuals and organisations that have contributed material for this book is long and exhaustive, but without them I would not have been able to compile the information and images necessary to complete it.

I especially thank Andy Parr for his extensive knowledge of the ambulance service in Sussex and for the use of many of the photographs from his own collection covering the ambulance services from East Sussex. Roger Leonard for images from his BAPS Heritage Collection, the now defunct East and West Sussex Ambulance Service's and members of the respective retirement associations. Thanks to the South East Coast Ambulance Service NHS Foundation Trust for donating their entire archive of photographs from the Sussex Ambulance Service Trust, which became a part of SECAmb in July 2006 with the amalgamation of the three services covering Kent, Surrey and Sussex. Also the various St. John Ambulance and Red Cross units throughout the county, especially the Chichester Horsham, Crawley and Southwick Divisions.

I am indebted to all the members of the public and ambulance service staff, whether retired or still serving, who have dug deep into their photo albums and contributed many of the images contained in this publication, and then scratched their heads to recall details of their past service and of the people, vehicles, buildings and events concerned. They include: Graham Lincoln, Valerie Lee, Len Barrett, Francis Blencove, William Foster, Barrie Nicholson, Eric Huntington, Gary Peasey, Richard Dyer, H.K.Moody, Roger Leonard, Elizabeth Arthur, Brian Knight, Mrs. Wilfred Virgo, Bob Catt, Nigel Smith, Linda Underwood, Janet Greener, Brian Prevett, John Layhe, James Type, Rod Green, Martin Guarnaccio, Tim Fellows, Ron Parsons, Tina Start, Sally Gander, Mark Plaine, Brian Bastara, Roger Saych, Bob Read, Mike Herriot, Peter Wells, Chris Rose, Brian Jones, Mike Newbold, Tony Cottingham, Roger Greenaway, Karen Ditton, Sheila Hilton, Kevin Poile, Steve McIntosh, Steve Woods, Roy Nightingale, Bob Franks, Nigel Hammond, Keith Marshall, Floss Mitchell, Sandra Spinner, Tim Gorringe, John Walker, Bob Morris, Gary Edwards, William Pike, Stuart Neave, Haydon E Ebbs, Terry Blackman, Victoria Burtenshaw, Neville Bettley, Arthur Dunmall, Andy Brian, Sheila Hilton, Harold Lovelace, Mrs. E Arthur, Barbara Chapman, Edward Bell.

Also the staff at East Sussex Record Office, Royal Pavilion & Museums, West Sussex County Archive, Bognor Local History Society, Littlehampton, Newhaven, Henfield and Steyning Museums, Hastings Local History Society, Sussex Police Museum, the Canoness of St. Augustine in St. Leonard, Slaugham Archive Collection, The First World War in East Sussex project, West Sussex Photo Memories, Rocky Media Archive, The Ambulance Heritage Society, and the Observer Series of Newspapers and the West Sussex County Times for information gleaned from their many publications.

I would like also to thank Nick and Linda Shepperd of Woodfield Publishing Ltd for their help and expertise in publishing this book.

My apologies to anyone I have inadvertently omitted to mention.

Brian Janman, March 2020

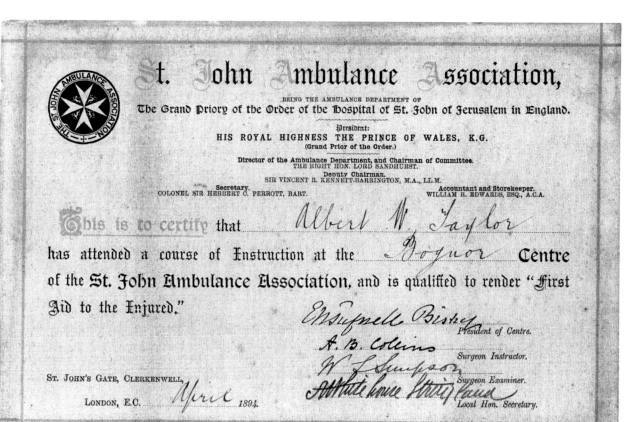

Certificate awarded to Albert Taylor by the Bognor Regis Centre
of the St. John Ambulance Association in April 1894.

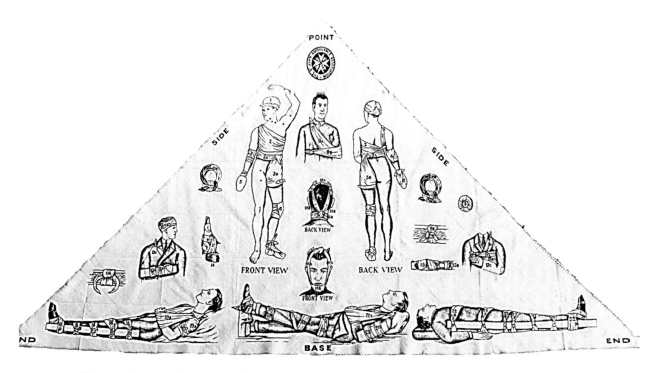

Illustrated triangular bandage from an early St. John Ambulance Association first aid manual.

The Early Years

Worthing St. John Ambulance Association

Members of the St. John Ambulance classes have just passed their annual examinations held at St. Andrews School, Clifton Road. For the third year in succession the whole of the male members have successfully passed. This must be most gratifying to Dr H. Leeds Harrison, who for two years has instructed them

Dr. J. H. Smith of Hove, the examiner, paid the male members a great compliment by stating that as a class it was the best he had ever examined. The female members were instructed as usual by Mrs. W. S. Simpson; twelve gaining certificates.

Extract from a Worthing newspaper dated 1896.

Eastbourne St. John Ambulance Railway Division volunteers with a wheeled stretcher circa 1900. Note the St. John Ambulance Association banner hanging behind the men and the first aid box in the foreground marked 'Eastbourne Station' and carrying the Cross of St. John. At the time many railway companies had first aid teams made up of station employees.

Old newspaper cutting depicting a wheeled ambulance litter belonging to Arundel Hospital circa 1900.

EAST SUSSEX COUNTY COUNCIL

TECHNICAL INSTRUCTIONS

HAYWARDS HEATH CENTRE

A COURSE OF SIX LECTURES ON
AMBULANCE

Wil be given in

Mr. BANNISTERS SALE ROOM, MARKET PLACE

Commencing 7pm

TOMORROW, WEDNESDAY, FEBRUARY 21st
ADMISION FREE

An examination will be held at the end of the Course.
Successful Students will be presented with the Certificate
of the St. John Ambulance Association.
Intending Students are requested to send their names to
the local Hon. Secretary Mr. H. Attree, I Clifton Terrace,
Haywards Heath.

Extract from the Mid-Sussex Times, February 20th 1900.

AMBULANCE WORK AT BEXHILL

PUBLIC MEETING AT THE VICTORIA HALL

ST. JOHN AMBULANCE DIVISION TO BE FORMED

A public meeting was held at the Victoria Hall on Tuesday evening for the purpose of considering the advisability of forming a division of the St. John Ambulance Brigade.

At present some 16 volunteers, all trained and possessing ambulance medals and certificates have come forward to form an Ambulance Brigade, but they are like workmen without tools. There is a strong feeling in the town that, with a small public effort, all equipment could be easily provided and an Ambulance Corps formed, supplying a real and useful want of the town.

These volunteers have already found an Ambulance Surgeon – Lieut. Col. Wallis, and they have elected a committee to enquire as to the best appliances to procure, considering local conditions. In considering the type of ambulance and the cost of the same, the most efficient equipment is the horsed ambulance. This is a covered van of the 'bus' type, on four wheels, fitted with two racks and two stretchers with telescopic handles. In plain varnished wood, on good springs the cost would be about £75. It should be supplemented with, the committee think, a Furley stretcher at £1 17s 6d, bandages, splints, dressings, diagrams, sundries etc. say £10, total say £90. To this amount uniform and maintenance must be added. In considering this type, the matter of horsing and storing came under consideration. The committee succeeded in finding a job master who would undertake to horse and harness the van any hour of the day or night at the rate of 6s to Hastings Hospital and back, 10s to Battle Infirmary and back and for town work at proportional rates. With regard to storage, the Committee wrote to the Town Clerk. They have been offered been offered a spacious loft in the Town Hall Yard where all the appliances and material could be kept together and where the brigade could drill etc. and the van housed and cleaned for the sum of £15 per annum.

After a prolonged debate on the matter a motion was passed to support the formation of a St. John Ambulance Division in the town, and the appointment of the committee was approved.

Extracts from the Bexhill-on-Sea Observer, Saturday 1st February 1902

AMBULANCE VAN FOR BEXHILL

Ever since the Bexhill Branch of the St. John Ambulance Brigade has been in existence, it has been very much in need of an ambulance van. For some considerable time, donations and public subscriptions have been solicited, and now the local branch have in their possession a van of a modern type. It has been built by Messrs. Atkinson and Phillip of Newcastle, and is fitted up to carry two stretchers and attendants. It is built of walnut and has two windows on either side and runs on rubber tyred wheels. It is now available for use, and although additional internal fittings have to be made, and the Brigade hope, as soon as it is complete, to give the public an opportunity of seeing it by having a parade or by giving a demonstration.

We might state that the Brigade has been greatly helped in procuring the van by the generosity of Sir Edward and Lady Ermyntrude Malet, who gave a handsome donation towards the van, which cost between £70 and £80. The Bexhill Hospital Committee also gave grants, and for the past three years the proceeds of the Tradesmen's Hall have been devoted to the cause.

Extract from the Bexhill-on-Sea Observer, Saturday 9th December 1905.

The Horsham St. John Ambulance Association, formed in 1906 by six railway workers, initially held its classes in a platelayers hut in the marshalling yard at Horsham Railway Station, but was later given permission to use a waiting room at the station. There was no organised ambulance service; the only transport available for invalids in the town was a wheeled litter which was borrowed from the local volunteer fire brigade. The West Sussex County Times reported on a public meeting held at Horsham Town Hall on June 26th 1926 when it was agreed to form a division of the St. John Ambulance Brigade in the town, and at the next meeting, held on July 6th, 30 qualified first aiders gave their names. In 1938 the Division was holding its meetings in the town hall and the ambulance was then kept in Jackson's Garage in Springfield Road. There was no accommodation for the duty crew, who waited for calls either by the garage telephone or on the corner of the Bishopric. The Division was able to build its own headquarters building in 1938.

Men of the Hastings St John Ambulance Brigade photographed in front of their new horse-drawn ambulance in 1906. The vehicle was built by Messrs Davis and Son, coach builders from Battle, and was described as 'Being a distinct improvement on the brigades former two wheeled stretcher'. The Division was formed on August 11th 1902 under the direction of Superintendent W. E. Jenner and Dr G. Locke.

THE BRIGHTON POLICE AMBULANCE

The remarkably quick time in which the Brighton Police Ambulance appears on the scene of a street accident or at a fire when serious injuries necessitate it must be, to some people, a matter for wonder. In the recent collision between cabs resulting in injuries to two elderly gentlemen in North Street, no more than five minutes could have elapsed between the receipt of the telephone message and the arrival of the vehicle for the removal of the injured to the Sussex County Hospital.

How is it done? Well, there is an ingenious arrangement at the Preston Circus Fire Station. The telephone message is received, and by simply pulling a lever in the Fire Station, the doors of the coach house and stable immediately open, the horse, upon whom collar and harness fall automatically, is ready to be attached to the ambulance, while simultaneously the gates giving exit to the roadway fly open, the ambulance being on its way in less than a minute from the time a call is received.

At night too, the stable yard is at the same time lighted up by a powerful arc electric lamp, also from the single pull of the lever in question. The system is that of ropes and counter-weights, and is ingeniously applied as for the Fire Station itself by Superintendent Lacroix.

Extract from the Brighton Gazette and Hove Post, August 15th 1907.

CUCKFIELD RURAL DISRICT COUNCIL

HORSING AMBULANCE

THE COUNCIL INVITE TENDERS FOR HOUSING AND HORSING A DISINFECTING VAN and for HORSING THE COUNCILS AMBULANCE for the year ending 30th September 1911.

Separate tenders may be made for the Horsing of the Ambulance.

Tenders on forms to be obtained of me, to be sent to me on or before 29th September Instant.

Council Offices
  Haywards Heath

G. H. WAUGH
Clerk to the Council

20th September 1910.

Advertisement from the *Mid-Sussex Times*, 20th September 1910.

Copy of an old newspaper cutting showing the Horsham Boys Brigade with their 'walking ambulance' circa 1910.

The Bognor Men's Detachment (Sussex 47) of the British Red Cross Society soon after its formation in 1911.

The Littlehampton Branch of the St. John Ambulance Association was formed at a meeting held at the towns Auction Mart on Thursday July 29th 1897. The town's St. John Ambulance Brigade was formed some years later, and became officially registered on November 12th 1907, with Mr. A. W. Harris being elected to be its first Superintendent. The division's first uniformed public duty was at the opening of the new Norfolk Bridge on the 27th May 1908. The division later acquired an Ashford Wheeled Litter at a cost of £16.00, and are seen here parading along Surrey Street with it circa 1911.

The newly formed Chailey Detachment of the British Red Cross Society (Sussex 54) circa 1913.

Men of the Littlehampton St. John Ambulance Division with an early Box Kite aeroplane, August 1913.

1914-18 – The Great War

A ladies Red Cross Voluntary Aid Detachment (Sussex 66) was established in Ditchling in July 1913 with a membership of five officers, 22 members and two cooks. Their training began at a Field Day in Falmer, and, early in 1915, the detachments first patients arrived at Ditchling's Red Cross Hospital, established by the Vicar, Reverend Norton, in a pair of houses in Lewes Road.

A Red Cross Society field training day, 1913. Sussex 54 VAD (Chailey) together with Sussex 78 VAD (Worthing) staged a base hospital in Stanmer Park, Falmer, treating 'wounded' men from two companies of the Lewes Territorials.

NEW MOTOR AMBULANCE FOR BEXHILL

For a town which is situated some 4 miles from the hospital the provision of adequate facilities of transit is of the utmost importance. Hitherto Bexhill has been served in this matter, and also for the transport of invalids, by the horsed vehicle of the Bexhill Ambulance Brigade, which has proved of greatest value, and by a convertible motor ambulance owned by Messrs Pulham & Co. of Sackville Road.

This service will now be greatly improved by a new and finely equipped motor ambulance which has been made for Mr. Pulham, and which may be hired for the purpose of removing invalids or hospital cases. A handsome enclosed car has been specially adapted as an ambulance, the stretcher being conveniently arranged on one side, extending from the back of the space by the side of the driver. An opening at the back enables the patient to be placed inside and removed in a reclining position without the least effort or inconvenience. There are two seats inside for nurses. The interior is hand- somely upholstered, while the make and arrangements ensure perfect ease and comfort. Another advantage is that the outward appearance of the motor ambulance is like an ordinary car.

Mr. Pulham has already received orders for the use of the motor ambulance from Hastings and other places in the neighbourhood, and the fact that the town now possesses such an up-to-date vehicle is known to be widely appreciated.

From the *Bexhill-on-Sea Observer*, 27th June 1914.

Per 6D. Mile

FOR HIRE

MOTOR LANDAULETTES
∴ and TOURING CARS ∴

Silent Knight
Daimler Ambulance,

1/- per mile.

SPECIAL TERMS FOR LONG JOURNEYS.

DRIVING TAUGHT.

H. Pulham & Co.

27, SACKVILLE ROAD, BEXHILL.

'PHONE No. 399.

Officers and men of the Hastings Division of the St. John Ambulance Brigade standing in Castle Hill Road in August 1914. The photograph was taken shortly before twenty men from the division left for Devonport and service with the Royal Army Medical Corps.

Ambulance Brigade Mobilized

Chichester has cause to be proud of its Division of the St. John Ambulance Brigade, twenty-one of whose members left on Friday afternoon for service at Davenport and the Channel Islands. Only Privates have been called so far, and these 21 left by the 2.35 train with the hearty good wishes of the Mayor, Councillor S. A. Garland JP, the Superintendent of the Division, Admiral Holland JP, Sergeant F. J. French, and the other officers who, with many of the citizens, assembled at the railway station to bid them farewell.

Such veterans as Private H. Holder, well known as 'the handy-man' and Private Cotterell of Shopwyke, were among the party who answered to their country's call.

Extract from the Observer and West Sussex Recorder, August 12th 1914.

Ambulances bringing soldiers wounded at the Battle of the Marne to the war hospital established at the Brighton, Hove and Sussex Grammar School in Grand Parade, Hove in 1914.

Men of the Brighton Quadrilateral Division of the St. John Ambulance Brigade photographed with their horse drawn ambulance in 1915. The division was first registered in June 1915, and most of its members, together with members of the Brighton & Hove Red Cross unit, joined the local Voluntary Aid Detachment to assist with transporting wounded soldiers from Brighton railway station to the many war hospitals situated in and around the town. They reportedly moved over 35,000 casualties between 1915 and 1919, and also established a rota for air raid work.

A Joint War Committee Ford Model T ambulance in Hastings during the Great War.

Military ambulances at the Filsham Park War Hospital in 1915. The hospital was established at the Convent of Our Lady, St Leonards-on-Sea, in 1914.

The convent, built in the grounds of Filsham Park Estate, was opened in 1909, and nurses from Voluntary Aid Detachment Sussex 16 were stationed there between 1914 and 1917.

The first wounded to arrive were 35 Belgian soldiers in October 1914. There were no further intakes until January 1915 with the arrival of 30 British wounded, mostly convalescent cases that had previously been treated at No2 Eastern General Hospital in Brighton.

Extract from an article entitled 'Autographs from a VAD Nurse: Filsham Park Hospital'

Nursing staff with an ambulance outside the Filsham Park War Hospital, circa 1915.

Members of both the Bognor and Chichester St. John Ambulance Divisions with an ambulance train at Chichester railway station circa 1915. The trains would bring wounded soldiers from hospital ships berthed at one of the south coast's ports to be transferred by ambulance either to Graylingwell War Hospital or one of the other smaller war hospitals in the area. Note the ambulance visible in the left background.

Pictured on the same occasion as the photo above, St. John men, soldiers and railway staff at Chichester railway station with the same ambulance that can be seen in the background in the previous image.

Red Cross nurses and recuperating soldiers at Hickwells Convalescent Home, Chailey, in 1915.

In the afternoon of Friday 15th September the motor ambulance, purchased by public subscription raised by Dr. Locke J.P. through an appeal in the Hastings and St. Leonards Observer, was brought to the Town Hall and formally inspected outside the Queens Road entrance by the Mayor (Aldermen G. Hutchings J.P.), who wore his robes, and was attended by the Macebearers and accompanied by the Deputy Mayor (Councillor Perrins) and members of the Council. His Worship examined the interior and exterior of the new equipage, and expressed his appreciation to Dr. Locke.

The new ambulance will prove a valuable acquisition to the property of the Hastings Corps of the St. John Ambulance Brigade. Several members of the Corps and some representatives of the Girl Guides were in attendance.

Extract from the Hastings and St. Leonards Pictorial Advertiser September 21st 1916

Presentation of a Ford Model T ambulance to the First Aid Nursing Yeomanry (FANY) circa 1917
This ambulance was paid for from funds raised by the Horsham & District branch of the British Farmers Red Cross Fund. Trained FANY nurses served all over the western front from 1916 onwards both as ambulances drivers and in first aid posts immediately behind the front lines.

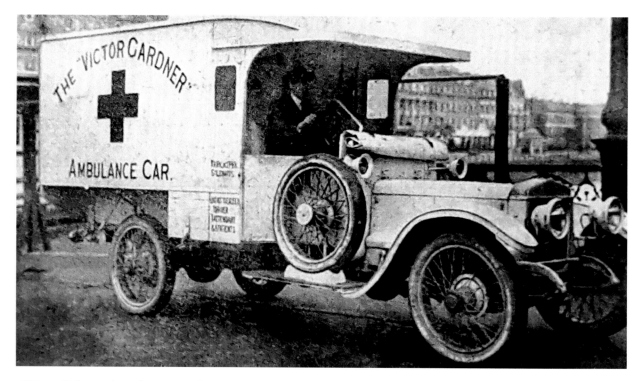

This ambulance, based on a Daimler 60hp car chassis, was donated by a local businessman to the Hastings and St. Leonard's branch of the Red Cross in February 1918 in memory of his son who was killed in Flanders in 1917.

Bognor Red Cross men and local dignitaries with two Ford Model T ambulances in Bognor High Street, Saturday 4th September 1915. They were taking part in a British Red Cross Society fund-raising day in and around the town to raise money to buy ambulances for service on the Western Front. A total of £218.12s.6½d was raised on the day.

WW1 ambulance donated by the Midhurst branch of the British Farmers Red Cross Fund circa 1917.

The Littlehampton St. John Ambulance Division was formed in 1908 and during the Great War its members formed part of the local VAD unit. Five of the division's members, including what appears to be a young new recruit, are pictured here circa 1918 with the towns Joint War Committee's Bean ambulance.

MOTOR AMBULANCE BOUGHT

The new motor ambulance for Bexhill has been bought. It is a forty horse power N.E.C. A first class bus body will be built and the total cost when it is on the road will be about £500. About half that is in hand, and three or four local gentlemen have guaranteed the overdraft. It is hoped to raise this by the time the body is built, which will be in about 10 weeks.

Extract from the Bexhill-on-Sea Observer, May 4th 1918.

Joint War Committee ambulance outside Sussex 53 VAD depot in Davigdor Rd, Hove circa 1918.

The Inter-War Period

The British Red Cross and the Order of St. John had formed the Joint War Committee early in the 1914-18 war to provide help to the armed services medical units. In 1919 they appointed a Home Service Ambulance Committee to set up a scheme to help the sick and injured in the UK.

This committee arranged for serviceable ambulances returned from the battlefront to be reconditioned in the Red Cross's own workshops. The Committee planned for County Directors to administer the scheme in their areas on a trial basis, but it soon became clear that a permanent service was needed, and ambulance stations were set up across the nation, equipped with these reconditioned vehicles, and crewed by trained volunteers.

What became known as the Home Ambulance Service became this country's first nationwide ambulance service. The ambulances were originally painted black and usually, but not always, carried both Red Cross and St. John wording, often written either side of a red cross on a white circle.

There were no national standards for newly built ambulances, and local coachbuilders built bodies on a variety of English and foreign chassis to meet their customers' specifications. Neither was there any national legislation covering the provision or standards of ambulance services, and it was often the urban or district councils, in conjunction with the voluntary aid societies, which funded and operated their own local services. These would usually be under the supervision of the relevant councils Medical Officer of Health, with the voluntary aid societies providing the crews to man the vehicles. In several cases in Sussex the local Police operated the ambulances, again with the assistance of Red Cross or St. John members.

BOGNOR MOTOR AMBULANCE

Sir, - It would be interesting to know who is responsible for the good order of the Bognor Motor Ambulance.

My son met with a serious accident on Friday evening, May 9th, and he was treated by the doctor on the same night. On the next day, Saturday, the doctor ordered him to Chichester Hospital, but to my surprise the motor ambulance was still out of order, and had been so for a fortnight, and no one seemed to know who is responsible for its repair.

Consequently my boy had to be taken in the horsed ambulance, which caused him much pain, and I believe undid what good had been temporarily done by the doctor and us overnight.

Is it not a scandalous shame that ratepayers' property should be found to been broken down for a fortnight, and to cause such inconvenience when required for such an urgent case. I think that those on whom the responsibility rests shirk that responsibility; is it not time that figure-heads be replaced by competent officials?
Yours Truly,

J. TITCOMB   4, Southover Road, Bognor

Extract from the Bognor Observer and West Sussex Recorder, 21st May 1919.

The Bexhill-on-Sea St. John Ambulance Division was formed at a meeting in the Victoria Hall on Tuesday 28th January 1902. The extract below from the Hastings & St Leonards Observer describes how it obtained its first motor ambulance in 1919.

BEXHILL AMBULANCE SYSTEM

I wonder how many of us in Bexhill realise that there exists in our town, without any effort on our part, a very efficient organisation which holds itself in readiness, night and day, to come to our aid should one of us be the victim of an accident or other calamity necessitating our safe and speedy removal to hospital. Yet for years past such a society has been unostentatiously working in our midst under the name of the Bexhill Ambulance Brigade. And of all the various members of this society, from the two skilled surgeons at its head down to the least important brigade man, not one has been actuated in his work of mercy by any other motive than the alleviation of suffering in some shape or form.

job masters etc., it will easily be understood what heart breaking delays sometimes occurred. In some cases as long as three to four hours would unavoidably elapse between the call and the arrival at hospital.

In 1916 it was decided to endeavour to obtain an up-to-date motor ambulance, and a fund was started to defray the expenses. This was uphill work at a time when the demands on the public generosity were mainly on account of the war. The Brigade, however, worked manfully at the task and, to its credit and without the support of any municipal grant, by its own efforts reached the total of £572.

Meanwhile the Brigade had been fortunate enough to purchase a splendid car at an

Bexhill's first motor ambulance, a 40 horse power N.E.C.

Until the year 1916, the Society had been more or less content to use as a means of transport what was then considered a very neat and well equipped little ambulance bus which was drawn by a horse in the good old fashion way. There were some, however, who were not content, and foremost among them were the doctors, who, best of all, knew the vital importance, in many cases, of a few minutes lost or gained. And when we consider that, owing to the difficulties of keeping horses always ready, and the cost of their maintenance, it was found necessary to trust to obtaining them, when required, from local

almost nominal figure, and with the addition of a new body designed to meet their requirements, they possessed before the summer of 1919, one of the finest motor ambulances in the country, the total cost of which only amounted to between £600 and £700.

By the end of 1919 this amount was almost achieved, but, unfortunately, there have been many heavy and unavoidable expenses in connection with the ambulance. It is hoped, however, that the town of Bexhill will realise what a boon is theirs, and will determine to set it free of debt by the end of 1920.

MOTOR AMBULANCE SCHEME IN SUSSEX
MR.F.H.WAYNE SAYS IT IS DOING A MOST USEFUL WORK
MEETING AT HAYWARDS HEATH

As many of our readers are aware, the British Red Cross Society is developing fresh activity in Sussex by means of the Home Service Ambulance Scheme. Its main objects are :- (1) To place a motor ambulance within a radius of not more than 15 miles from every house in Sussex, ready at call to attend all cases of accident or illness requiring transport, at a very moderate scale of fees per mile. (2) To aid the Ministry of Pensions in conveying disabled sailors and soldiers to the various hospitals in which they require treatment.

Last Tuesday afternoon a meeting of the Haywards Heath & District representatives was held at the Parish Room, Church Road, (by kind permission of the Rev. E. Cresswell Gee). Mr. Godfrey Hooper (Commandant) presided, and a deeply interesting address was given by Mr. F. H. Wayne (Assistant County Director for Sussex). The scheme, he said, was inaugurated last April with the idea of trying it for 12 months as an experiment, and he thought he could say it had been doing a most useful work – most important, perhaps, in the country districts. Of course they had some stings, one of the greatest objections being that it was an experiment, but his answer to that was that life was composed of experiments! Others said they were not interested until they knew what other counties were doing. But suppose everybody said that! The thought was too terrible.

The objections seemed so futile that they were hardly worth considering. His reply to them was to give the scheme a fair chance, and everything would go right. He admitted the scheme could be improved upon. Giving particulars of the work of the cars in Sussex, the different areas of which were shown by a coloured map, Mr. Wayne pointed out that cars had been placed in West Sussex at Chichester, Storrington (for Pulborough), and Horsham, while in East Sussex they were at Battle, Eastbourne, East Grinstead and Haywards Heath. In addition the Lewes and Brighton ambulance cars were cooperating in the scheme, so that every house in the county, with the exception of a small part of the Rye district, was within 15 miles access of a car. During 5 months the car at Eastbourne carried 449 patients and covered a mileage of 1,367; that at Horsham carried 22 patients and ran 715 miles in eleven weeks; 20 patients were carried and 135 miles covered in six weeks by the Chichester ambulance; while at East Grinstead, during a period of 14 weeks, 20 patients were carried and 535 miles covered. The Haywards Heath car, which was only delivered in December, had already carried 25 patients and journeyed 432 miles.

The statistics of the work of the cars were not records of joy-rides but records of magnificent service for the benefit of the community (hear, hear). Haywards Heath was one of first places which was decided on for a centre for a car, and he should like to pay a compliment to Mr. G. Hooper, Miss Cooper, Mr. T. Chandler and Messrs. Hampton, who had been the mainstay of the work locally

The speaker also said that no serious difficulties had arisen, and they were in no sense competitors with anybody. They were not out for a profit or to compete with any garage man who could carry a case. One of the main objects of the scheme was to help necessitous cases. His the thanks were due to garage proprietors who had housed their cars free of charge. Offers had doubled the number of cars they had, which spoke highly for the garage proprietors, who were not in Sussex for their health, but for business.

General O'Brien proposed a very hearty vote of thanks to Mr. Wayne for his able address. He had explained the scheme very carefully and told them their duty. He (the speaker) was sure that each one of them in the room had only the one idea, and that to make the scheme a success in their own district. They wanted the scheme in its entirety to work for the good of the community, and if this were done the small places would benefit accordingly.

Extract from an article in the *Mid-Sussex Times*, 30th March 1920.

Chichester & District Motor Ambulance

The Chichester & District Motor Ambulance completed its first year of usefulness and work on Monday, November 15th last. During the past year 141 patients have been carried, the motor ambulance having covered 2,044 miles, as besides the local journeys within the allotted area several special journeys have had to be taken as far as London, Folkestone, Netley and Brighton.

Nearly all the cases have been critical and urgent, requiring immediate and careful removal, and it is gratifying to know that no deaths or accidents have occurred during the course of the work.

There are fifteen voluntary motor drivers and twenty-seven stretcher bearers registered with the Committee, to all of whom the very heartiest thanks are due for the splendid and ready assistance they have given, especially to those who have so frequently turned out at a moment's call, night or day in all weathers, to help in the alleviation of suffering.

The success in both the management and the prompt answering of calls for the ambulance is very greatly due to the arduous work so kindly undertaken by Mr. Earnest Hooper, and the able and ready assistance of Superintendent Brett and his staff at the Police Station.

The committee responsible for the management of the Chichester & District Motor Ambulance, which is worked in conjunction with the County Home Ambulance Scheme of the British Red Cross Society, consists of Miss Hannah, Mr. W.L. Gibbins JP, Admiral Swinton Holland, Mr. E Hooper, Superintendent Bret and Lady Garland,

Extract from the Chichester Observer & West Sussex Recorder, November 24th 1920.

St. John Ambulanceman Jack Drewett with the Hastings St. John Division's Renault ambulance in the early 1920's.

HAYWARDS HEATH AND DISTRICT MOTOR AMBULANCE

December 22nd, 1923.

Please Note:

That on and after the above date the ambulance will be stationed at Griffin's Garage, Haywards Heath. Phone 23.

Thos. H. CHANDLER,

Hon. SECRETARY

From the Mid-Sussex Times, 25th December 1923.

The presentation ceremony for Chichester's new ambulance held in Priory Park on December 24th 1924. The ambulance, a silver-grey 18hp Buick supplied by Fields Garage of Chichester, was fitted with bodywork by May and Jacobs of Guildford and was given to the city by Lady Bird. It replaced an earlier Ford based vehicle.

BEXHILL AMBULANCE BRIGADE

MORE SUPPORT NEEDED

The report of the Committee of the Bexhill Ambulance Brigade, which will be presented at the Annual Meeting at the Town Hall on Thursday March 19th, states:-

The Brigade continues in a satisfactory state of efficiency both as regards its members and appliances. As so many of our poorer townspeople are moved either without charge, or at a reduced charge, the Brigade must continue to appeal to its friends and supporters for financial assistance. Subscriber's letters can be obtained from the Hon. Treasurer, one for each 5s subscribed, available for twelve months. Hearty thanks are tendered to the Mayor and Corporation for the use of the Town Hall for lectures, etc., and to the Hon. Auditor, Mr. A. E. Wood.

Our thanks are due to the late Mayor, Councillor E. W. C. Bowrey, for presiding at our Annual Meeting, for the kind interest he has taken over the affairs of the Bexhill Ambulance Brigade, and for the donation he obtained from the Borough Council, which has enabled us to pay our previous liabilities of £137 7s. 2d. and to start 1925 free of debt having provided the Brigade new uniform, which was badly wanted, and having renewed all stores at all stations, leaving a balance of £47 12s. 9d. It is hoped that we shall be able to provide the Brigade with new overcoats during the year, which are much needed.

The total donations received was disappointing, being only £268 13s. 6d (including £100 from the Borough Council) which is a small total from the 20,000 inhabitants of Bexhill and district, in reply to the 1,200 appeals that were issued, in addition to two appeals in the local papers. Any person may at any moment require the use of an ambulance for himself or his friends. It is evident that an ambulance is a necessity to Bexhill, to take patients to Hastings Hospital, and that if sufficient donations are not received all idea of keeping it maintained by voluntary subscription will have to be dropped and an annual appeal wll have to be made for public funds, to pay for the necessary upkeep.

It is estimated that a sum of £300 should be sufficient for the annual upkeep of the ambulance and the Brigade. The charges made for the ambulance are at times criticised for being too high, but it must be remembered that these have to cover the running expenses of a first class ambulance, the chauffeur's wages, the pay to bearers, the upkeep of the brigade and the supply of first aid stores at six stations.

All casualty cases are carried free of charge, and all persons who have not the means to pay anything are either let off altogether or asked to pay as much as they can afford, while all cases can obtain letters worth 5s each in part or whole reduction of charges. During 1924 the ambulance was called out 123 times, and of these nothing was received from 24 cases and 4 were dealt with by letters.

Our thanks are due to the boys of Reginald Road School who delivered the 1200 appeals sent out, free of any charge, and when pressed to receive some remuneration, said that they did it for the good of the town, and wished anything given to them to be presented to the Ambulance Brigade funds, which was done. Our special thanks are due to the £100 donation from the Borough Council, £5 5s from the Battle Board of Guardians, £4 6s. 1d from a concert arranged by Mr. Christian, £5 from the Tradesmen's Ball, £14 4s from the Bexhill Hospital Fund, £3 from the Bexhill Bowling Club, £3 from the Bexhill Charity Cup Competition, £1 5s from the Hastings and St. Leonards Football Club, and £5 from St. Peters Church.

A most interesting and instructive series of ambulance lectures was given by Dr. Murdoch during October to December. The class was not so large as usual, and the members much appreciated the ability and kindness of the lecturer in preparing them for the examination. Of the eleven candidates all passed, two for certificates, one for medallion and eight for labels. The examiner especially congratulated the lecturer and the class on the excellence of the results of the examination.

Extract from the Bexhill Observer, March 1925.

HEATHFIELD & DISTRICT AMBULANCE COMMITTEE

Mr. F. Howard Martin was largely responsible for the provision of the ambulance service. He organised a series of fund raising events at the Recreation Hall, and these events were always of a very high standard.

The first ambulance, a Morris, was purchased in 1925 and a trust was formed to supervise maintenance and manning. The Fire Brigade and the Ambulance Committee were closely allied, the personnel of each being practically the same.

Members of the Fire Brigade sold ambulance tickets to people in Heathfield and Waldron parishes; the tickets were also available in shops. They cost 1/- and entitled a husband, wife and children under 14 to free use for a year on a Doctor's Certificate. Thousands were sold. The price went up to 1/6 after four or five years, but the same services were provided.

The firemen attended lectures and knew the rudiments of first aid but were not affiliated to either the Red Cross or the St. John Ambulance Brigade, so the vehicle carried a white cross on a red background. For the first three or four years the rate of pay for the driver and attendant was 1/6 per hour, but this was only paid when they were called away from work, otherwise it was voluntary.

When the Morris ambulance deteriorated it was replaced by a Packard, and finally by a Sunbeam Talbot, of which they were rather proud.

The ambulance was moved to the coach-house of the Heathfield Hotel at the onset of World War 2 when the Fire Station had to be kept manned and suitable accommodation provided for the men on duty.

Extract from 'Cross in Hand' by Francis Ford.

Uckfield Home Ambulance Service's Austin ambulance in the mid 1920s.
It had black bodywork by Pilcher Green Ltd. of Burgess Hill.

The Hastings St. John Ambulance Division's Napier ambulance circa 1925.

The Daimler ambulance operated by Moody's Ambulance Service, Pulborough, taking part in what appears to be a procession in the village circa 1925.

The service, later re-named the Pulborough & District Ambulance Service, was formed in the early 1920s by Mr Moody, the owner of Moody's Garage at the foot of Church Hill where the ambulance was garaged.

Photographed at the Corporation Yard in Waterworks Road, where the town's ambulances were garaged, this is Hastings town's Austro Daimler ambulance in 1926.

Horsham SJAB Private Edward George Chase standing alongside the first motor ambulance to be operated by Horsham Police. The vehicle was presented to the town by Mrs M. Laughton JP in September 1926. Built on a Morris Commercial chassis, its overall yellow colour scheme and usage for infectious cases soon gained it the nickname 'The Yellow Peril'.

This is the first motor ambulance to be operated by the police in Worthing. It was gifted to the town by Mr. H. Aaron from Angmering–on-Sea in 1926.

1928 newspaper image of the 6 cylinder Minerva ambulance operated by the Bexhill-on-Sea Division of the St. John Ambulance Brigade.

Two Austin ambulances operated by the Brighton Police in 1928.

Hastings St. John Division's Ford Model A ambulance circa 1929. Originally painted in the St. John Ambulance Brigade's usual black colour scheme, the vehicle now carries the grey paint scheme adopted by the Town Council when they took over the operation of the service.

Worthing Police Officers with their newly acquired No2 ambulance in 1929. Paid for by public subscription, it was built on a Dennis 30cwt chassis by Caffyns of Horsham. The Shoreham Police also took possession of an ambulance at a ceremony held outside Shoreham Town Hall on Wednesday 12th February 1930.

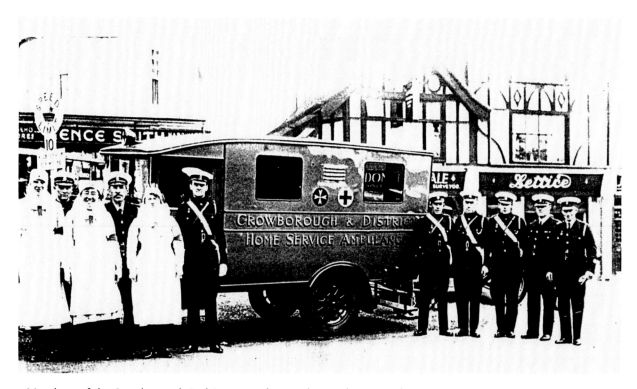

Members of the Crowborough Red Cross Men's Detachment (Sussex 17) and the Ladies Detachment (Sussex 46) with the Crowborough and District Home Ambulance Service's 10cwt, 16/32hp, Morris Commercial ambulance. It was purchased in 1930 for £361.15.0 plus the cost of fitting it out with equipment.

TOWNSPEOPLE'S GIFT TO POLICE

£1,000 UP-TO-DATE AMBULANCE

PARADE PRESENTATION SCENE

Referred to by the Lord Lieutenant of the County (Lord Leconfield) as 'a most magnificent present from the town of Worthing to West Sussex Constabulary', the new motor ambulance subscribed for by citizens and purchased for the Borough, was presented by the Mayor of Worthing (Councillor H. F. Carmichael) to the police on Tuesday afternoon.

The ceremony took place on the parade at the Pierhead in front of a large number of spectators and a smart patrol of local police. The gift was received on behalf of the police by Lord Leconfield accompanied by Mr. A.S. Williams, the Chief Constable, and other dignitaries.

The Mayor expressed his pleasure in presenting the handsome police ambulance for use in the Worthing Division. The gift incorporated the very latest practice in vehicles of the kind, he said, and was fitted with every devise and convenience that ingenuity could suggest for dealing with the removal of accident cases and the conveyance of private patients. The engine was by Dennis and the body had been built by Messrs. Caffyns – both firms of high repute. The inside of the ambulance was fitted up to deal with five stretcher cases, and it was equipped with an oxygen gas cylinder, splints, bandages and other medical and surgical accessories. There was a powerful floodlight on top to enable cases of night accident to be expeditiously and carefully dealt with.

"As you may suppose, an ambulance of this character costs a great deal of money," continued the Mayor. "And the amount required for its purchase - £1,000 – has been very generously subscribed by residents of Worthing".

To Save Life

"In these days, when there were so many bad motor accidents" said the Mayor, "it was essential that the police should be furnished with a vehicle of this kind so that every effort might be made to alleviate pain and save life. The ambulance would be available also for the removal of private cases to nursing homes and hospitals. There was a minimum charge of 5s in the borough and probably 1s a mile outside the borough. The ambulance was fully insured against every risk to the vehicle and the persons using it".

Extract from the Worthing Herald, 5th July 1930.

Bert Selsby, a member of the Aldingbourne Red Cross Detachment (Sussex 63), at a roadside first aid post on the A29 south of Woodgate level crossing in the early 1930's.

WORTHING'S GIFT TO PETWORTH

OLD AMBULANCE TO SPREAD GOOD WORK

POLICE PRESENTATION

Worthing's old ambulance, which was replaced by the magnificent new one presented in July this year, is to be given to Petworth.

The ambulance work at Worthing, which is undertaken by the police, is entirely voluntary and they have decided that it would be difficult to keep both vehicles running. The one to be given to Petworth was presented to Worthing in March 1926 by Mr. H Aron. It is fully insured up to March next, and is being overhauled and re-named. The police at Petworth have had consultations with the Vicar and Parish Council there and have arranged to take over Petworth Fire Station to garage the ambulance. It is expected that it will do useful work in the district as Petworth is on the main London to Bognor main road.

We understand that the presentation will be made next week.

Extract from the *Worthing Herald*, 29th November 1930

Annual inspection parade, Bognor British Red Cross Society Women's Detachment (Sussex 88) in the grounds of Bognor Hospital, May 6th 1931. South Bersted parish church, St. Mary Magdalene, in the background.

ST. JOHN AMBULANCE CENTENARY

◆

NEW MOTOR AMBULANCE FOR HASTINGS BEING BUILT

A new St. John motor ambulance is now being constructed which, when completed, will be far superior to either of the present cars. It will be smoother, faster in running and more silent, and every provision will be made for the patients comfort. The two cars now in use, a Ford and a Daimler, will be retained for emergencies.

A secondhand Rolls Royce chassis has been fitted with a saloon ambulance body and the work of painting and properly fitting it out for use is going ahead with all speed, but it will not be ready for the road until a few weeks' time. The exterior will be painted blue, while the interior is to be lined with blue washable leatherette. There will be two tip-up bucket armchair seats for the attendants. The engine is of the six cylinder type, developing 45 to 50 horse power.

The car will be fitted with four sliding windows enabling the patient to have an adequate supply of fresh air, which is often vitally necessary. Ventilation is also provided through the roof.

PATIENT'S COMFORT

Everything is done for the patients comfort. The wheels are fitted with shock absorbers, the chassis is elliptically sprung, and the stretcher is of the latest Rostillian pattern. A useful improvement is the provision of runners, which pull out from the back of the car, so that the stretcher can be pushed into the ambulance on a frame instead of being lifted in, as at present. This obviates any jolting of the patient.

Before being brought into use the car will be inspected by members of the Town Council and the medical profession, and will be dedicated.

The total cost of the car is £500, of which £150 is still required. A flag day, which is being held on July 11th, will help towards this, but money is also required for other purposes, such as the purchase of uniforms and the general running expenses of the brigade. Gifts of money or offers to help with the flag day would be welcomed by the Superintendent, G. H. French.

Extract from the Hastings & St. Leonards Observer, Saturday 13th June 1931.

THE NAPIER MOTOR AMBULANCE
of the Worthing Ambulance Division,
St. John Ambulance Brigade

Purchased by the money collected on
their FLAG DAY, 1ˢᵗ August 1931

The Mayoress, (Mrs H.F. CARMICHAEL, J.P.) had very kindly consented to hand over the Ambulance on the Broadwater Sports Ground, on SUNDAY, 25ᵗʰ OCTOBER at 3 o'clock, to Captain E.A. Chill O.B.R., MD., Assistant Commissioner for Sussex, Acting for the Commissioner of No.8 (Duke of Richmond's) District, E.A Richards Esq.

The Worthing Ambulance Division have pleasure in giving to their Subscribers and Friends a brief description of the NAPIER and its equipment.

The body had been partly rebuilt and renovated, and the engine thoroughly overhauled by Messrs. Rice & Harper Ltd., of Guildford, whose predecessors built the body a few years ago for the Guildford Division. The drivers cabin is enclosed, the driver's seat forming a locker in which are carried the full kit of tools and other equipment. Overhead are two cabinets containing several sets of splints. The body is heated, as and when required, by the engine. A large "AMBULANCE" sign is carried on the roof in front, and is lighted at night by three electric lamps.

Two stretchers are carried, and there is room for three sitting patients in addition to the attendants and driver. An Ambulance Sister will accompany all cases whenever possible. Double doors at the rear of the rear of the body open the full width; these doors open from the inside, the main entrance to the body being on the offside behind the driver's compartment.

THE INTERIOR is fitted with eight clear glass windows with spring-blinds; six windows may be opened, if required, at any time. On long journeys the invalids have a clear view of the country though which they are passing, while the blinds may be drawn to ensure privacy for the sick and injured as and when required. Lockers are fitted for blankets, sick-room utensils, and the "Eureka" First Aid Box. The permanent stretcher-carriage is fitted on the nearside, the stretcher having telescopic handles. A "Float-on-Air" PNEU-MATIC bed is attached to the stretcher, with a PNEUMATIC PILLOW to ensure comfort for the patient, free from jolting or vibration.

Amongst other equipment carried in the interior are two electric lights, speaking tube to the driver, fixed medicine cabinet, carry sheet, blankets, pillows, bowl, towels, hot water bottles, etc., and many other articles for the treatment, comfort, and convenience of the sick and injured.

It is interesting to note that the ambulance is equipped especially for dealing expeditiously with transport cases, or accidents at night. A powerful spotlight is carried on the off-side which may be focused on houses, paths, ditches and accidents in almost any position; at the rear, mounted on the roof, is another powerful spotlight, so that assistance may be rendered to the injured as readily and efficiently by night as by day.

The Ambulance is painted BLACK and WHITE - the colours of the St John Ambulance Brigade - with the EIGHT POINTED CROSS on the panels on both sides the vehicle.

Extract from the Worthing St John Ambulance Brigade's presentation leaflet, Sunday 25ᵗʰ October 1931.

Worthing St. John Ambulance cadets pose with a trophy in front of 'The Napier.'

CHICHESTER ST. JOHN AMBULANCE DIVISION REFORMED

The first meeting of the newly reformed Chichester Division of the St. John Ambulance Brigade was held in the council chamber on Friday last. The Mayor (Alderman W. H. Leggett) presided, and he was supported by Superintendent W. H. Brett D.C.C., Capt. E. A. Chill of Battle (the County Commissioner for Sussex St. John Ambulance Brigade), and Mr. Wigglesworth (the Divisional Secretary).

Others present included Alderman H. S. Ayhmore, Alderman J. R. Hobbs, Councillor C. G. Allen, Dr. Barford, Dr. Langhorne, Mr. W. J. B. Trotter, and Inspector Gee, who acted as Secretary. It was stated in the minutes that as the outcome of the previous meeting, 44 names had been handed in for membership, of which 23 had already passed for first aid.

FUNDS

Alderman Ayhmore, who was Treasurer of the old brigade, was asked to speak on the question of funds for the new division. He had very little to say on the matter, said Alderman Ayhmore. When the old brigade when into abeyance there were a certain amount of funds in hand. There were some War Saving Certificates purchased in 1927, and he did not know their present value.

The fund was vested in three trustees, the late Mr. Bastow, Mr. French and himself. There could be no parting with it without proper authority. He was in favour of re-starting the brigade, but these things where trustees were concerned had to be dealt with in a certain manner. He thought it would be best for them to appeal for funds in the ordinary way, and to write to him to know if these funds could be transferred to the new division, and he would call the old members together and get their views on the matter. Mr. Goldie moved, and Mr. Tremble seconded that "Application be made to Alderman Ayhmore as suggested" This was carried unanimously. Superintendent Brett suggested that the question of raising funds be left to the Committee to consider, and this was carried on the proposition of Mr. Trotter.

ACCOMMODATION

Mr. Brett said he had made enquiries about various halls which he thought might suit. He had heard from the Secretary of Education to the effect that it might be possible for them to have the use of the Lancastrian School Hall. After some discussion, it was moved that the offer of the Lancastrian School Hall be accepted.

SUBSCRIPTIONS

The next item on the agenda was "To obtain the views of the meeting as to any subscriptions that might be made by members".

Capt. E. A. Chill said he had been very keen all along to see another division in Sussex, and he was very pleased to hear that one was being formed in Chichester. With regard to subscriptions, it was perfectly open for them to pay a subscription or not pay a subscription. A few years ago, each member subscribed 7/6d. That did not supply uniform, as they came out of the general subscription, and cost about £5, which included an overcoat. The 7/6d was for stores such as splints, bandages and all little things for use in the division. At the present time, under the new Commissioner, they were not insisting on that 7/6d, as they found that most divisions were able to get all they wanted through subscriptions. There was no reason, he said, that they should be downhearted, and he wished them every success. It was finally decided, on the proposition of Inspector Gee, that there be a voluntary subscription of 6d a week.

THE LECTURER

On the proposition of Supt. Brett D.C.C., Dr. Langhorne was appointed as lecturer, and it was decided that the first class be held at 7.30 pm at the Lancastrian School Hall.

Mr. Bridle was appointed secretary for the lecturers. The following committee was formed: Messrs Weller, Goldie, Trotter, Watts, Hobbs, Hodgkinson and Roots.

A PRESENTATION

At this juncture of the meeting, the Mayor said it gave him the greatest pleasure to present Mr. Holder with a bar to his medal. Mr. Holder had served for 35 years in the brigade. He was almost looked upon as a handy man. He was very pleased to see him there that night. He had come up smiling to help in the formation of a new brigade, and he trusted that he would live long enough to get another bar to his medal. (Cheers)

Before the close of the meeting, Inspector Gee was asked to have charge of the division until such time as a superintendent was appointed.

Extract from the *Chichester Observer & West Sussex Recorder*, March 23rd 1932

Men of the newly reformed Chichester Division of the St. John Ambulance Brigade
outside the Lancastrian School, Orchard Street, Chichester, in 1932.

A page from an
information leaflet
issued by the Worthing
St. John Ambulance
Division in 1932.

Motor Ambulance Service.

· WM. C. TERRY,
Divisional Transport Officer,
" Reculvers,"
78 Broadwater Road,
Worthing.

Telephone,
Write
or Call.

Telephone—Worthing 1188.

The Motor Ambulances are sent out **fully equipped**
with driver and one, or two, members of the Division.

St. John Ambulance Sisters, or other Nurses, will
accompany invalids in the Ambulances.

The Ambulances are equipped with Pneumatic Beds and
Pillows and all requisites are carried for the comfort and
convenience of the sick and injured.

NO HEAVY LUGGAGE CARRIED.

Charges.

Although the work is carried out by Members **entirely
Voluntarily,** a charge has to be made to cover the heavy
expenses of running and maintaining the Ambulances.

Hailsham St. John ambulancemen in Market Square, Hailsham, on Sunday 27th November 1932 with the division's brand new motor ambulance, a 19 hp Morris. It was given to the division by Mr. and Mrs. Arthur Jarvis, and had cream and brown painted bodywork mounted on rubber blocks for patient comfort.

HELP FOR THE INJURED

FIRST AID HUT OPENED AT
GUESTLING

Mts. Joyce opened a new St. John Ambulance First Aid Hut at the top of White Hart Hill, Guestling, last Sunday.

The hut, which was constructed by Messrs. De Laine and Heighton of the Hastings Town Division, is a veritable roadside hospital. It includes a first aid surgical outfit, splints, bandages and stretchers, and everything necessary for dealing with a possible accident at this dangerous corner. Water can be obtained at the White Hart Inn a few yards away and a public telephone booth is equally close. There is an emergency key on the door for the use of the public. Hastings ambulance men will be on duty there every Sunday from Easter until the end of September.

A short service of dedication was conducted by the Rector of Guestling (the Rev. H. R. Evers), and members of the Hastings Division paraded under Dr. D. Martin supported by Ambulance Officer Wren and Transport Officer Coleman; members of the Nurses Brigade were under Miss Coxeter.

The service commenced with the St. John hymn.

From the Hastings and St. Leonards Observer, Saturday 13th May 1933.

1930s information leaflet.

BATTLE AND DISTRICT
HOME SERVICE AMBULANCE
(BEDFORD DE-LUXE. 1936)

IN CHARGE OF

ST. JOHN AMBULANCE BRIGADE
(BATTLE DIVISION).

Ambulance Station :
56, High Street, Battle.

Telephone : Battle 200
Emergency : Battle Ambulance
(No Number).

GENERAL CHARGES

1/- per mile up to 50 miles ; minimum charge 3/-.

10d. ,, ,, from 50 to 120 miles ; minimum charge £2 10s. 0d.

9d. ,, ,, from 120 miles upwards : minimum charge £5.

When the journey involves staying away over the night, the charges for bed and breakfast for Driver and Attendants will be extra.

Mileage counted from Ambulance Station back to Station.

Nurse supplied upon request free of charge.

Barrett of Battle, Printer, 23, High Street.

Worthing St. John Ambulance Division's two Commer ambulances in 1933. PO 7268 was presented to the division in April 1933 by the town's Mayor, Mr T.B. Hawkins. BBP 24 had the bodywork from the old Napier ambulance, purchased from the Guildford St. John Ambulance Division in 1931, and rebuilt onto this new Commer chassis by Worthing SJAB members.

Lady Leconsfield and local dignitaries being shown the Petworth Police Force's new Ford Model A ambulance at a presentation ceremony held at Petworth House in July 1933. Crewed by Police Officers and members of the local Red Cross unit, it was paid for by public subscription and was garaged at Castles Garage in Park Road, Petworth.

Horsham St. John Ambulance Division's Lomas bodied 27hp Willy's Knight ambulance at the division's garage in Springfield Road in 1934. Purchased for £350 in 1929, this was the division's first motor ambulance, as previously they had helped crew the town's police ambulance.

A Sussex Red Cross member bandaging the hand of an injured cyclist on the side of the London to Brighton road at Pyecombe in 1935.

Midhurst's first motor ambulance was converted from a Morris car given to the town's Red Cross Detachment, Sussex 25, in 1932. The Officer in this 1935 photograph is probably Mr Melhuish, who ran the service until 1956, after which Cocking publican Vic Charman took over the running of the ambulance, which was kept in a garage in Grange Road.

Members of the Aldingbourne British Red Cross Detachment, Sussex 63, with their Morris ambulance, registration number HW 3588, on the forecourt of the Aldingbourne village school in 1935. Mr Hoad, on the left of this group of six, was a signalman on the Southern Railway, and was the unit's commanding officer. The ambulance was kept in the Silver Queen bus garage in Fontwell Avenue, and the unit held its meetings in the Labour In Vain public house at the junction of Westergate Street and Nyton Road.

The Henfield & District Ambulance Club's first motor ambulance on Henfield Common in 1935. The vehicle had been converted locally from a saloon car, which probably explains the highly unusual side door loading arrangements. It served the town until 1944 when it was replaced with a second hand Austin ambulance.

Littlehampton St. John Ambulance members with a blue liveried Austin ambulance in 1936.

This Morris 8 car was purchased in 1937 cost of £140 by the Uckfield branch of the British Red Cross Society.
It was used to provide first aid cover at some of the notoriously bad road junctions in the area.
Note the two folded Furley stretcher sticking up through the open roof.

Hastings St. John Division's Lomas bodied Vauxhall 25 circa 1937.

Worthing Police's brand new Austin ambulance delivered in September 1937.

1939 – 1948

In 1937 the British Government set up the ARP (Air Raid Precautions) service. Local councils were made responsible for organising the service in their area and for the recruitment of volunteer wardens, messengers, ambulance drivers, rescue parties and first aid teams.

At first the volunteers had no official uniform other than an ARP armband, but in October 1939 they were issued with blue overalls with a red on black ARP badge. The service was officially renamed as the Civil Defence Corps in 1941, and from May full-time and regular part-time wardens were employed and issued with a uniform consisting of a dark blue battledress and beret. Women wardens were issued with a four pocket dark blue serge tunic and skirt.

The auxiliary ambulances used by the ARP and Civil Defence units were very often local conversions of big salon cars or light commercial vehicles.

Littlehampton ARP wardens, St. John and Red Cross nurses taking part in the towns National Service Day parade on July 5th 1939.

Members of the Littlehampton ARP unit wearing anti-gas suits washing down the town's ambulance during a training exercise in 1939.

The Haywards Heath Woman's Detachment of the British Red Cross Society (Sussex 50) with the town's brand new Austin Big 6 ambulance at its dedication ceremony on 24th September 1939.

Members of the Hailsham St. John Ambulance Brigade with the division's Vauxhall ambulance outside their headquarters in Groveland Road, circa 1939. This refurbished First World War period wooden military building was purchased by the division's benefactor, Mr Jarvis, who had it erected on ground he had previously purchased for the division's use. The ambulance was later sold to the Eastbourne St. John Ambulance Division.

ARP first aid vehicles and Littlehampton's Austin 'Big 6' ambulance on Beach Road in 1940. Note the stacks of metal stretchers on the roofs of the two cars.

The St. John Ambulance Brigade and the Red Cross continued to operate alongside the ARP services during the war. This is the Rye St. John Ambulance Brigade's Lomas bodied Fordson ambulance circa 1940.

Above: Civil Defence personnel assisting a casualty into an auxiliary ambulance in Hastings, April 1942.

Left: A Worthing ARP party using a ladder as an improvised stretcher during a rescue exercise in February 1940.

Military personnel and Red Cross nurses in front of an army ambulance outside the Military War Hospital in Balfour Road, Preston, Brighton, during WW2. The nurse second from left is wearing the Mobile VAD unit armband.

Newspaper image of Bexhill-on-Sea's wartime ARP First Aid Party and their ambulances circa early 1940s.

Brighton **Woman's Auxiliary Police Service personnel** with one of the **Brighton Police ambulances in 1942.** The police continued to operate the service until the formation of the Brighton Borough Ambulance Service in 1948.

Southwick ARP members with their auxiliary ambulances c1944.

Above: Newhaven Civil Defence staff with a fleet of auxiliary ambulances circa 1943

Left: Bognor ARP First Aid Party members practicing on one of their own comrades circa 1943.

The sign in the back of the car reads 'Casualty Car 9'.

HURST AMBULANCE GARAGE WANTED

Dear Sir, We are in gross trouble over the activities of the British Red Cross Society in the district of Hurstpierpoint and Hassocks. The society in London have been good enough to allocate us an ambulance for use in the district; we have got all the helpers we require to operate and man the ambulance; the medicine officers who are kind enough to help in our work, say that they welcome arrival of a new ambulance, and that they have sorely missed the availability of an ambulance since the old one ceased to function.

But our trouble is that we cannot find anywhere to garage the new vehicle. It is an army type ambulance, and its overall length is 17ft 11inches. The height clearance must be at least 10ft, and the width is 7ft 7 inches. If any of your readers would be good enough to help us in this matter we should be most grateful and I am sure that they would be doing a great service to the district which we serve.

If possible, we would like to have the accommodation in or near the centre of Hurstpierpoint, as that will make it more efficient in its use.

Yours faithfully,

KATERINE M CAMPION

A letter to the Mid-Sussex Times, 12th December 1945.

The dedication ceremony for the newly formed Bognor St. John Ambulance Brigade's first ambulance, a converted ex-army Bedford, was held in the grounds of the Bognor Pavilion Theatre in October 1946.

Hastings Ambulance Service

The Mayor (councillor F.W. Chambers) inspected the St. John Ambulance headquarters at Phoenix Hall, Castle Hill Road, on Saturday and opened a garage recently constructed. With him were Dr G.R Bruce (Corps Surgeon), Corps Superintendent G.H. Wren and Corps Officer S.W. Ashdown. Among others present were other officers, ambulance drivers and nursing attendants.

The Mayor was told of the work carried on and was shown where the Medical Comforts Depot will be. This is to be opened in January, and from the depot, local residents will be able to hire for a small fee articles for use in the home for sick persons such as air cushions and bedside tables.

At an informal ceremony in the Phoenix Hall the Mayor recalled that one of the first things he did when he was made mayor was to open that hall, and now, in his second year of office, he had come to see the completion of what had been done, and to congratulate all concerned.

In the development taking place in their services, the perfect solution of their problems was to continue the spirit of voluntary service, supplement it and aid it.

Spirit of the Service

There will be some things which must be done by paid professional people, but he was quite sure that there was room in all their services for the voluntary helper. "It will be a sad day for this nation if ever all this work is done by people who do it just for their job." He declared.

In the first redevelopment of the National Health Service in this town they would continue to use the St John Ambulance organisation. They had got to maintain the spirit of the service to the nation, and it could be done by those whose job it was to do it, and it could also be done by people supplementing them.

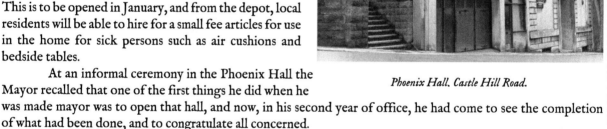

Phoenix Hall. Castle Hill Road.

The Mayor taking the inspection. The ambulances parked in the garage are: left ADY416, a Lomas bodied Vauxhall 25, and right BDY769, a Lomas bodied Bedford K series

Extract from the *Hastings and St Leonards Observer*, 30/11/1946.

Bognor Red Cross Society members with their carnival float 'War & Peace' at the East End car park, Bognor, in 1947.

St. John Ambulance, Grand Review of Sussex Divisions.

Worthing on Sunday afternoon (July 6th) saw one of the biggest parades since the war, when a grand review of the St John Ambulance Brigade Divisions from all over Sussex, over a thousand strong, marched through the town.

Before the parade moved off, the companies were inspected on West Parade, their assembly point, by the Chief Commissioner, Lieut-General Sir Henry Pownall K.C.B., K.B.E., D.S.O., M.C., the County Commissioner Mr David Bryce J.P., the Hon. County President, the Countess of Bessborough J.P., the Assistant Commissioner, Mr W. Trotten, the County Superintendent, Miss D. Hubbard and the County Cadet Officer, Miss M. Trill.

The Divisions, led by the Hastings band, followed by the officer in charge, then marched past the Town Hall, where the salute was taken by Lieut-General Sir Henry Pownall, supported by other high-ranking officers of the Brigade, and the Mayor and Mayoress, Aldermen and Councillors.

The parade, after passing the saluting base, made its way to the Assembly Hall via Wenban Road and Stoke Abbot Road, where a service was conducted by the Mayor's Chaplain, the Rev. H. J. H. Humprey and addressed by the Rev. H.W. Janisch. The following Divisions took part in the parade along with Cadet and Cadet Nursing Divisions from across the county:

The Chief Inspector, Lieut-General Henry Pownell, inspecting a Nursing Cadet Division

AMBULANCE DIVISIONS

No1 Company: Worthing, Henfield, Horsham and Crawley.
No 2 Company: Southwick, Lancing, Portslade, Rye, Littlehampton and Lewes.
No 3 Company: Hastings, Eastbourne, Robertsbridge, Chichester and Hove.
No 4 Company: Brighton Corps, Brighton Town, Seaford, Bexhill and Shoreham.

NURSING DIVISIONS

No 5 Company: Worthing, Hailsham, Chichester and Hastings.
No 6 Company: Roedean, Eastbourne, Hastings and Brighton.
No 7 Company: Hove, Lewes, Portslade, Bognor Regis, Moulscombe, Patcham and Rye.
No 8 Company: Henfield, Seaford, Horsham, Lancing, Littlehampton, Steyning and Preston.

Extract from the Worthing Gazette, July 9th 1947.

1948 and the Introduction of the NHS

Section 27 of the National Health Service Act 1946 made local authorities responsible for the provision of the ambulance service in their area. They were authorised to do this either by direct provision or 'by making arrangements with voluntary organisations or other persons for the provision by them of such ambulances, transport and staff'.

East and West Sussex County Councils and the County Boroughs of Brighton, Hastings and Eastbourne all elected to take the later course, and delegated the responsibility for the provision of the service to the voluntary aid organisations. In effect this meant little change as far as the general public were concerned, as the voluntary organisations simply continued to do what they had been doing previously. The major change was in the funding arrangements, with the County and Borough Councils now being responsible for funding the service.

In East Sussex it was the various Red Cross units who provided cover in the more rural areas, while in the larger conurbations of Eastbourne, Brighton and Hastings it was the St. John Ambulance Brigade. In West Sussex it was in the main the St. John Ambulance Brigade. In all the services a number of full time ambulance drivers and attendants were employed to man the vehicles both by night and day, backed up by unpaid volunteers, mainly at evenings and weekends.

Both the St. John and Red Cross services operated under what was known as an 'Agency Agreement', effectively operating on behalf of the local authorities and being paid by them for the services provided. Day to day operations were controlled by each separate service, but overall responsibility for the provision of the service lay with the
county and borough authorities and came under the auspices of their respective Chief Medical Officers.

An evening dedication ceremony for Bexhill's new Spurling bodied Bedford K series ambulance in 1948.

Hove Ambulance Service

At the time of the 1948 NHS Act coming into force the ambulance service in Hove was provided by Hove Borough Council using directly employed staff, unlike many other towns in East Sussex, who used the St. John or Red Cross on an agency basis. In 1966 the service was transferred to the East Sussex County Council, still with directly employed staff.

The services vehicles were painted in a two-tone grey colour scheme, and accommodation was provided in a wooden building within Hove Borough Council's yard at 149A Old Shoreham Road. This building was replaced in the 1950's with a brick built eight bay garage with offices and crew rooms on the first floor. One constant problem was that with the ambulance station having been built in the council yard, crews had to constantly battle with other council vehicles, including dust carts, for parking space.

Hove operated its own control manned 24 hours a day. It would take bookings for admissions, discharges, transfers and outpatient appointments directly from local doctors and hospitals, but all 999 calls were routed through from either Brighton Police control room, Brighton Borough Council Ambulance Service control or from the East Sussex County Council control in Lewes. Hove control would then allocate these calls on to a Hove crew. Hove crews only used their radios, which were on the same frequency as the rest of East Sussex, while on emergency calls. At all other times communication with the Hove control room was by telephone. This arrangement lasted until a central control was opened in Eastbourne by the East Sussex County Council Ambulance Service.

Like many services, Hove attracted ex-servicemen into its ranks, and one such was the Superintendent-in-Charge, a Mr Alex Calder, who, pre-war, had been a policeman in Hove. He joined the Royal Air Force and became a bomber pilot with 617 squadron, the famous 'Dam Busters'. He became a Squadron Leader with 617 squadron, and led the squadron on highly successful raids on German railway installations, dropping 10 ton 'Grand Slam' bombs that brought down the Bielefeld viaduct, thus destroying a vital rail link, and on the heavily fortified V1 and V2 rocket assembly sites in Germany. Other staff members included ex fighter pilots, Royal Marines, tank commanders and paratroopers. With these kind of backgrounds, the crews had a confident manner and were able to put up with the less than ideal facilities. They earned the nickname 'Calder's Cowboys', which they carried with pride.

Hove staff worked a 46 hour a week contract, working one night, two late and two early shifts over five day period. Up until the early 1960's Hove crews wore a black uniform with a blouson jacket, similar in style to that worn by the British Army, along with a black beret. This uniform style was replaced in the 1960's with a naval style double breasted jacket and peaked cap, changing again to blue when the counties ambulance services were unified in 1974.

Eastbourne's maroon painted ambulances in 1948. The vehicles were purchased and operated by St. John Ambulance Brigade under the agency agreement with the town's Borough Council.

Lewes St. John Ambulance Brigade's Austin K2 based ambulance photographed in the late 1940s. Many of these vehicles were converted from ex Auxiliary Fire Service vehicles after WW2.

A brand new Bedford ambulance outside Coomb's Motors in Norman Road, St. Leonards, in November 1948. The two men in the centre are Hastings St. John man Fred Dodson and Hastings Corporation's full-time ambulance driver Trevor Bailey.

Above: Parked outside the old Swan Hotel in Pulborough in 1949, and behind the two cars in the centre of the photograph, is the Pulborough St. John Ambulance Division's. Austin Welfarer ambulance. It was common practice at the time for St. John members to stand by at crossroads, such as this one at the junction of the A29 and A285, most summer weekends and Bank Holidays.

Right: A Lomas bodied Bedford K Series ambulance operated by the Red Cross in Hurstpierpoint circa 1950.

Below: The dedication service for the Bognor St. John Ambulance Division's new Austin Welfarer ambulance held in the grounds of the Bognor Pavilion Theatre in 1950.

Brighton staff based at the old ambulance station to the rear of Brighton General Hospital circa 1950.

AMBULANCE TEAMS MOST
SUCCESSFUL YEAR

The Borough of Worthing Ambulance Division, St. John ambulance Brigade, was second in the Brigades Annual Competitions held at the Central Hall, Westminster, on Saturday July 5th 1952.

The team received the runners-up award, the Symonds Eccles Challenge Cup, from the Duchess of Gloucester, Deputy Commandant-in-Chief of the Nursing Corps and Divisions. They scored $250^1/_2$ marks, $15^1/_2$ marks behind Wolverton (Bucks) and three ahead of Shrewsbury, who were placed third.

The Worthing team was: Divisional Officer W. Virgo, Corporal J. Thompson, Private F. Long and Private C. Carlton, with Private G. McCourty as reserve.

For the team test they had to treat a young man who had 'fallen' from the top of a cliff to a ledge and sustained a fractured skull and a compound fracture of the right leg. They were allowed 15 minutes for their demonstration, which included climbing up to a realistic cliff ledge, passing up splints, bandages and all other necessary materials, and removing the injured man when treated.

Extract from the Worthing Gazette, 7th July 1952.

Sidney Phillips, Fred Pearce and Fred Manbridge of the Arundel Red Cross Men's Division (Sussex 41) with the units Austin 'Big 6' ambulance in 1954.

Hastings Ambulance Service's annual inspection, 1954

From left to right the vehicles are an ex RAF Thornycroft lorry used as a major incident equipment vehicle, a 1940 Lomas bodied Bedford K Series ambulance, a 1948 Bedford K Series with Spurling bodywork, a 1946 Austin K2 with Lomas bodywork, a 1938 Austin 'Big Six' with bodywork by Startin, a 1954 Bedford CA with Martin Walker bodywork, a 1937 Vauxhall 25 with Lomas bodywork and lastly an Armstrong Sidley saloon car used for sitting case patients.

Brighton Borough Ambulance Service's Bedford A series ambulance circa 1955.

Sussex St. John divisions at their annual parade on The Green, South Terrace, Littlehampton in 1955.

The fleet at Rye Ambulance Station circa mid 1950s. A re-bodied ex WD Austin K2 on the far left, an Austin Welfarer in the centre and a Lomas bodied Bedford K series on the right.

Rye St. John ambulancemen and nurses with the same Austin K2 ambulance, GWX 211, as shown in the photograph above.

Austin Welfarer ambulances operated by the Hailsham St. John Ambulance Division circa 1955.

Brighton's new ambulance station in Elm Grove on a misty day in the mid 1950s. Against the far wall are a
number of sitting case vehicles with London taxi cab style bodywork. In the garages are an Austin Welfarer,
six Bedford K Series ambulances and, nearest the camera, a single Bedford A Series.

A large crowd watching members of the Horsham St. John Division giving a rescue and
first aid display featuring a mock building collapse circa mid 1950's.

The Sussex based St. John Melody Makers 5 piece dance band circa mid to late 1950's

Members of the Chichester St. John Ambulance Division in 1956 outside their base in Coombes Yard in The Hornet with the units Austin Sheerline ambulance.

St. John ambulancemen at the old Lewes Ambulance Station in Timberyard Lane in the late 1950s. Harold Loveless, who went on be the Station Officer at Newhaven Ambulance Station, is second from right. From L/R the ambulances are a Bedford CA, a Daimler DC21 and two Spurling bodied Bedford A Series.

A Brighton Ambulance Service Bedford J series ambulance at a fire on Brighton seafront in the late 1950s.

Hailsham St. John Ambulance Division's Bedford A series ambulance in the snow in the late 1950s.

Harold Selmes, John Brockhurst, Tony Golding, Derek Matt and Tony Hoad in the late 1950s outside Russells Garage in London Road, Bexhill, where the town's St. John Ambulance Division's ambulances were garaged and maintained.

John Brockhurst later became the Deputy Chief Ambulance Officer for East Sussex Ambulance Service and Tony Hoad later became the Station Officer at Battle Ambulance Station.

The ambulances are a Lomas bodied Bedford K Series and a Barker bodied Daimler DC27.

Crawley St. John's Ambulance men with three of the division's ambulances, a Rolls Royce and two Bedford A Series, circa late 1950s.

Radio control of ambulances in West Sussex was first introduced in the Bognor Regis and Chichester area in 1957, the system being extended to both the Worthing and Horsham districts soon after. The use of mobile radio sets in the ambulances meant that crews no longer had to telephone their respective controls after each journey, and that they could be quickly dispatched to any emergency that arose while they were still on the road.

Alan Burbridge operating the radio at CHICAM Control based in the Chichester St. John HQ in The Hornet.

Superintendent Wilf Virgo mans the control desk of WORHAM Control, based at Worthing St. John Division HQ at 'Candia' in Farnscombe Road.

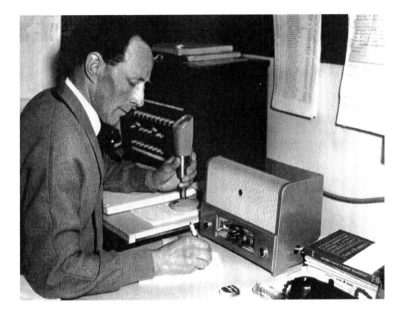

St John staff on duty at HORAM Control, based at Horsham St John's HQ in Orchard Street.

Brighton Borough Ambulance Officers and staff circa 1958. Chief Ambulance Officer Edward Sumter is siting sixth from the right in the front row, immediately behind the large trophy.

Transferring a casualty from a RAF Thorney Island based 22 Squadron's Westland Whirlwind rescue helicopter to a Brighton based Bedford A Series ambulance in East Brighton Park circa 1959/60. 22 Squadron had a Search & Rescue flight based at Thorney Island from 1955 to 1971.

The Men's Division of the Littlehampton St. John Ambulance Brigade with two of their ambulances circa 1960.

Bexhill's Barker bodied Daimler DC27 circa 1960. These vehicles were designed for the London County Council Ambulance Service but also served with many other services across the country. The chassis was built as low to the ground as possible to assist in the loading of patients, and, due to their well ballasted floor, they gave patients and crew alike a very smooth ride.

Eastbourne Ambulance Service's maroon painted Lomas bodied Austin Sheerline in the early 1960s.

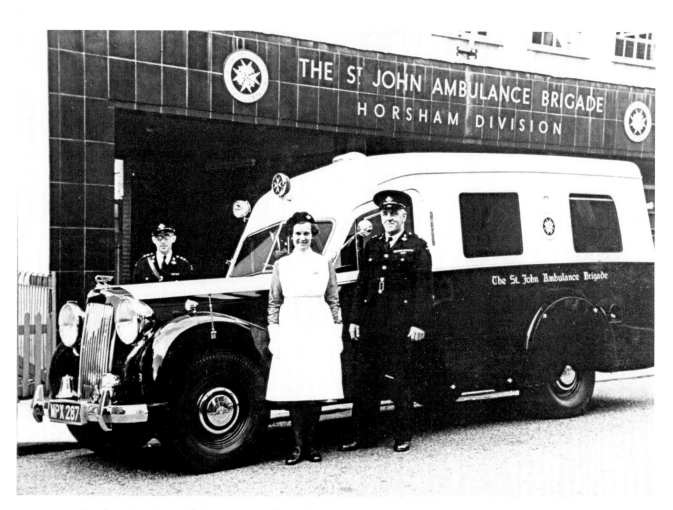

Horsham St. John Ambulance Division's Park Royal bodied Austin Sheerline ambulance circa 1960.
Standing in front of the ambulance with the nurse is George Denyer, the division's Cadet Superintendent, with Mr. Cottingham, the Divisional Officer in the background. Their divisional headquarters in Park Street was opened in July 1936 by Her Grace the Duchess of Norfolk.

Awaiting the start of The Worthing Borough Celebrations circa early 1960s are Worthing St John's Ambulance men dressed in vintage uniform with the division's preserved vintage wheeled litter.

Petworth St. John Ambulance Division's Bedford A Series ambulance in 1961. It was garaged in a wooden shed next to the Petworth Town Council offices in Station Road.

Mr. Vince Glover was appointed Chief Ambulance Officer for West Sussex County Council in 1961.

It was his initial responsibility to complete a comprehensive survey of the provision of the ambulance service in the county and make recommendations to the council in this respect.

His conclusions were that a more cost effective and efficient service could be provided by one directly controlled by the County Council using a combination of St. John Ambulance and Red Cross volunteers and directly employed staff.

C O P Y

LM   MINISTRY OF HEALTH

                                            Savile Row,

                                                 London W.1.

Please address any further
communication on this subject   Telephone: REGent 8444.
to THE SECRETARY   ext. 114.

Your Ref: B1/CH19.CH8/iB
M/Health Ref: LA(AMB)694/16976/3.   29 May, 1962.

Sir,

            National Health Service Act, 1946
            Section 27 - Ambulance Service

        I am directed by the Minister of Health to refer
to your letter of 23rd February, 1962, and subsequent
correspondence, and to say that, in view of the assurance
given by representatives of the Council to his officers
on 28th December, 1961, that the fullest possible use will
be made of voluntary effort, he hereby approves the proposals
forwarded therewith, modifying those approved by the
Minister on 28th April, 1949, as subsequently amended, for
carrying out the Council's duty under Section 27 of the
National Health Service Act, 1946.

        The Minister would be glad if the Council would
arrange for a copy of this letter to be sent to each of
the bodies who were entitled, under Section 20(2) of the
Act to make recommendations for the modification of the
proposals.

        The Minister would be glad to receive a further
three copies of the new proposals.

            I am, Sir,
                Your obedient Servant,

                (Sgd) T.B. WILLIAMSON

                    Assistant Secretary.

The Clerk of the West Sussex
    County Council,
County Hall, CHICHESTER

Mr Glover's recommendation was put to the Minister for Health by the County Council and approved by the MOH in this letter dated May 29th 1962.

The newly opened headquarters of the Southwick Division of the St. John Ambulance Brigade in 1963 who, at the time, were still providing the ambulance service for the area under the County Council's agency agreement. This building in the Twitten replaced their earlier headquarters in Watling Lane.

The Southwick St. John Division was formed at a meeting held at Hove railway station in 1929 and by 1930 its members were manning the Shoreham Police Ambulance. The division went through a series of name changes in its early years; at one time it was the Southwick, Shoreham & Portslade Division, before finally reverting to its original title of Southwick in 1946. The first ambulance the division owned was an Arrol-Johnson, obtained from the Bexhill Division in 1942.

The two Bedford CA ambulances on the left were purchased by the Chichester Division of the St John Ambulance Brigade in 1963 in preparation for the forthcoming changes in the provision of ambulance services in West Sussex. They are parked on the forecourt of the division's garages in Velyn Avenue, along with a Land Rover and an ex Civil Defence rescue unit.

1963: the County Council ambulance services

A ceremony held on March 31st 1963 in the grounds of County Hall, Chichester, marked the change-over of ambulance provision in West Sussex from the St. John Ambulance Brigade and the Red Cross to the newly formed West Sussex County Council Ambulance Service.

Members of both the St. John and Red Cross were on parade along with staff from the new County Council service. They were addressed by Mr Peter Mursell, the leader of the County Council, who thanked the St. John and Red Cross for the past 15 years of service.

The Duchess of Norfolk, President of the Sussex Branch of the British Red Cross Society, Captain J. M. Hodges, County Commissioner for the St. John Ambulance Brigade and Lord Robert Neville, County President of the St. John Ambulance Brigade were also present.

East Sussex County Council also took over the provision of the ambulance service in East Sussex from the voluntary organisations in 1963. The exception to this were the three Borough Councils of Brighton, Eastbourne and Hastings, who continued to operate their own independent services

Mr Peter Mursell, the Duchess of Norfolk, Lord Robert Neville and Captain J. M. Hodges inspecting staff from the new County Council Ambulance Service.

The inspection party and a number of new County Council ambulances.

Left: West Sussex County Council Ambulance Service's Worthing area control 'WORAM BASE' in Farncombe Road, June 1963. Station Officer Wilf Virgo takes a phone call while Head Driver S. Beatty passes a message over the radio.

Below: Hastings Ambulance Service's Deputy Chief Officer Mr. Fred Dadson in the services control office at Phoenix Hall, Castle Hill Road in 1963.

At the beginning of the West Sussex County Council's directly operated ambulance service Crawley was the only town in the county to have a modern ambulance station. This was built in Exchange Road in 1961, initially for the use of the town's St. John Ambulance division, but it was taken back into direct control by the council in 1963, as seen in this 1965 photograph showing two Wadham bodied BMC J2 ambulances in the garage.

Elsewhere in the county, and unable to make use of the existing ambulance stations owned by the St. John Ambulance Brigade, the County Council service initially operated out of temporary accommodation while brand new facilities were designed and built.

This hut in the grounds of County Hall in Chichester, was one of the temporary ambulance stations provided by West Sussex County Council. As well as being the base for Chichester's ambulance staff, it housed the counties ambulance control, CHICAM BASE.

The chap washing the back of an ambulance is Alan Ware, who later went on to be the Divisional Officer for the Chichester, Bognor and Midhurst Division.

Members of the Lewes St. John Ambulance Division with their newly
acquired Wadham bodied BMC LD ambulance in the early 1960s.

In 1963 West Sussex County Council ambulancemen Chub Weston (above left) from Crawley
and Pat Weeks from Horsham won the annual National Ambulance Proficiency Competition at
their first attempt. They won the best team, best attendant and best driver tests to take the
overall title, the first time ever all the trophies had been won by a single team.

Hastings Chief Ambulance Officer Mr George Plummer in his office in Phoenix Hall in 1963.

Brighton Ambulance Station staff circa 1963

Front row L/R: Charlie Genin, Harry Beer, Peter Spanton, Vic Martin, Gordon Sparks, Fred Mitchell, Eric Carey, Danny Hayes. Back Row L/R: Alfie Redman, Johnny Streeter, Joe Berry, 'Rusty' Grimley, Ted Giles, Ted Elliot, Frank Hurley, Bob Foden, Peter Marsden, Ted Williams.

Lord Newton, Parliamentary Secretary to the Minister of Health, on a visit to the newly built Midhurst Ambulance Station in Bepton Road on September 16th 1963.

Bexhill Staff based at the old Ambulance Station in Amhurst Road in 1964. Standing in front of a Bedford A series ambulance are Tony Hoad, who later became Station Officer at Battle Ambulance Station, John Watson, Peter Hathaway and Rowland Manktelow.

Hastings' 1964 Wadhams bodied Bedford CA, a dual purpose vehicle primarily used for sitting cases.

Right: Hastings St John ambulanceman Tony Poile (on the left) and his crewmate assisting an elderly patient into their ambulance circa 1965.

Felbridge & East Grinstead St. John Ambulance Division's BMC LD111 ambulance in 1965.

Hastings ambulancemen Tony Poile (right) and crewmate Wally in front of their ambulance on the day they won the Regional Ambulance Crew of the Year Award c1965.

Tony was the driver and Wally the attendant.

Above: A Westland Whirlwind helicopter of 22 Squadron from RAF Thorney Island and men of the Chichester St. John Ambulance Division giving a display in Priory Park during the 1965 Chichester Carnival.

Above: Hailsham 1965. A 1965 registered Bedford J1, DAP 161C, and a pre-1961 registered Bedford CA, DJK 967, which is still in St John livery two years after the county council take over. The ageing Morris J type ambulance in the centre is an ex Hove Ambulance Service unit awaiting disposal.

Right: Brighton ambulance staff at Elm Grove Ambulance Station in 1965. Those shown include Vic Martin, Norman Stoner, Alan Bunny and Edward Bell.

Haywards Heath Ambulance Station in Bridge Road circa 1966. It was built by East Sussex County Council in 1957 and was taken over by the West Sussex County Council Service in 1963.

Chichester's new ambulance Station in Summersdale Road opened in 1966. The crew facilities and the county ambulance control office were on the ground floor, with offices for the station and area officers on the first floor. The large garage could hold eight ambulances.

Bognor Regis's new ambulance station in Chichester Road opened in 1966. Like many of the new buildings constructed by West Sussex County Council during this period it was built utilising a system of modular, prefabricated, steel frame, concrete block and glass panels known as the SCOLA System (the Second Consortium of Local Authorities).

A BMC J2 on the forecourt at the newly opened ambulance station in Moat Lane, Worthing in 1966.

WEST SUSSEX AMBULANCE OFFICERS IN 1966

Back row L/R: Bill Parsons (Head Driver Pulborough), Harry Shurety (Station Officer Crawley), Vic Charman (Head Driver Midhurst), Stan Linsted (Control), Bill Mills (Head Driver Littlehampton), Allan Ware (Station Officer Chichester), Sid Lacey (Head Driver Bognor Regis), Harry Burton (Head Driver Shoreham), Ted Ayres (Station Officer Horsham)
Front row L/R: Wilf Virgo (Area Officer, Worthing), Doug Arthur (Control Officer), Graham Tilley (Admin Assistant), Mr. Vince Glover (County Ambulance Officer), Pat Weeks (Staff Officer), Oscar Lake (Chief Control Officer), George Wheatland (Area Officer B Division).

Burgess Hill's new ambulance station in The Brow under construction in 1967.

Lewes ambulancemen Mr R. Tapp (left) and Mr B. Clay won the county Ambulance Efficiency Competition at Battle last weekend and will now represent the County Ambulance Service in the regional ambulance competition at Battersea Park, London.

Cutting from unknown newspaper dated 23rd June 1967.

Three newly delivered East Sussex County Council Bedford J type ambulances on the forecourt of Mansfields Garage, Lewes, in the late 1960s displaying the red county crest bearing six gold Martlets and crown.

Chichester St. John Ambulance Division's brand new Wadham bodied BMC LD111 ambulance in 1968.

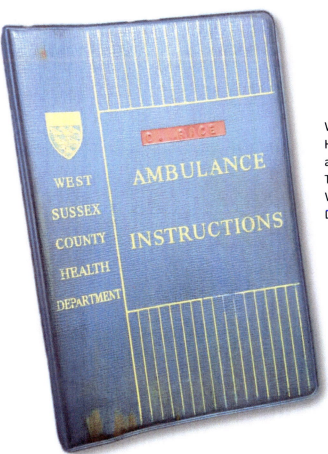

West Sussex County Council Health Department's ambulance instruction manual. This one was issued to Worthing ambulanceman David Rice in September 1968.

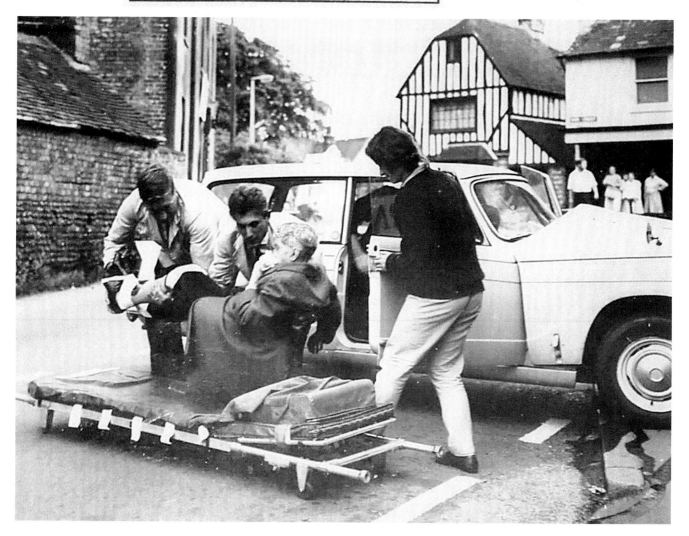

If you . . . . . .

LIVE IN SHOREHAM-BY-SEA
OR SOUTHWICK

LIKE DRIVING

HAVE A KNOWLEDGE OF OR ARE
WILLING TO LEARN FIRST AID

the vacancy for

AMBULANCE DRIVER/ ATTENDANT

can provide a worthwhile career of service to
the public.

Basic wage £15.8.4 a week (less 13s. 4d. a week without a
current first aid certificate) plus standby allowances.
Uniform provided.

Apply to County Medical Officer of Health, Metropolitan
House, Northgate, Chichester, for further information. Closing
date 10th March.

(c

Recruitment advert
published in the
Worthing Gazette
on February 26th
1969.

Ambulancemen Geoff Gander and Tony Hoad lifting a patient onto an old style Lomas
stretcher at a minor traffic accident in Old Town, Bexhill, in the late 1960's.

Hastings Ambulance Station in Bohemia Road soon after opening in 1969.

East Sussex Area Health Authority ambulancemen Ian Colwell and B. Jupp, winners of the
National Ambulance Efficiency Competition finals held at Stoke Mandeville Hospital in 1969.

AMBULANCE SERVICE 1969

Officers and Staff of the Ambulance Service:

Chief Ambulance Officer: E. R. KIMBER, A.I.A.O., F.I.C.A.P., F.I.C.D., A.M.R.S.H.

Deputy Chief Ambulance Officer: K. A. Williams

Superintendent Control: S. A. Charlwood, G.I.A.O.

Superintendent Training: C. Relf, G.I.A.O.

Station Officers: J. Thom, A. Bunney, C. Donno, G.I.A.O., A. Mackay, F. Hurley

Leading Ambulancemen: V. Martin, P. Spanton, R. Foden, A. Redman, P. White

41 Ambulancemen, 12 Ambulancewomen, 2 Clerk Typists

The number of patient journeys covered by the directly operated Service was 104,127, an increase of 6,439, which together with 6,902 patient journeys covered by the H.C.S. (a decrease of 246) brought the total patient journeys covered by the whole Service to 111,029, a total increase of 6,193.

The directly operated Service covered 362,905 miles (an increase of 11,381 miles) (extra ambulance 102 in 1969), and the miles run per patient journey was 3.6.

Compared with 1968, increases and decreases are as follows:

Increases				*Decreases*				
Accident and Emergency...	...	610		Inter Hospital	...	...	...	19
Mental	...	31		Maternity ...	...	...	...	74
Hospital to Home	...	115		Infectious ...	...	...	...	7
Treatment and Returns ...		2833		Others ...	...	...	...	178
Downsview Training Centre	...	1381		For Other Authorities	...	...		26
18 Club	...	1674		Night Sitters and Geriatric Visits				74
Health Dept O/T	... ...	86						
Day Nursery	...	220						
Total increases	... ...	6950		Total decreases	...	...		378

Retirement of Mr. A. J. Sumpter

July brought about the above. Mr. Sumpter was appointed as Chief Ambulance Officer when the Service was first formed in 1948 under the National Health Service Act of 1946.

He had the very difficult task of guiding the Service through its teething troubles in the early years, and in 1958-59-60 Brighton Ambulance Service made its mark in the First Aid world by winning National Trophies and followed this by being the first Ambulance Service in the country to set up its own graduated Training School. 1968 saw the pinnacle of his service career when he was made President of the National Association of Ambulance Officers. Unfortunately, dogged by ill-health during his final years, retirement proved a blessing in disguise, and his Deputy, Mr. E. R. Kimber, was appointed as Chief Ambulance Officer.

Heart Ambulance

Autumn saw the 'launching' of the above, which had been ready for many months but awaiting additional equipment that would put it on the 'Emergency Doctor' network as well as being on the Ambulance radio frequency. The £1,300 worth of special equipment includes battery-operated Defibrillator with an Invertor Unit to step the current up to 110 volts, battery-operated Cardioscope, mains/battery operated Cardiostatt, Laryngoscopes, Bronchoscopes, Automatic Resuscitator, and a multitude of lesser items vitally necessary to any medical team engaged in a life-saving operation. This has been called a 'mobile hospital' and perhaps is a portent of 'things to come'. Records of use are being kept, but a full year's work will be necessary before any true evaluation can be made.

Extract from the Brighton Borough Ambulance Service's annual report for 1969.

The Brighton Cardiac Ambulance and the Beginnings of Extended Training

Doctor William Parker, the Medical Officer for Health for Brighton Borough Council, under whose auspices Brighton Borough Ambulance Service operated, became aware that in Belfast, Northern Ireland, an ambulance scheme had been developed to safely transport heart attack victims to hospital.

Previously the norm had been to treat heart attack patients at home with up to five weeks bed rest, as it was a common misconception among doctors that many patients died while being transported to hospital. The Belfast scheme involved an ambulance being fitted with battery operated monitoring and defibrillation equipment, kept charged by an inverter on the vehicles 12 volt electrical circuit.

The crew of the Belfast cardiac ambulance included a qualified doctor and nurse in addition to the two ambulancemen. It was, in essence, what we would now term as a patient retrieval scheme. Dr. Parker decided to introduce this style of scheme to Brighton in 1970 and had one of Brighton Borough Ambulance Service's Bedford J1 ambulances fitted out with the bulky monitoring and defibrillation equipment.

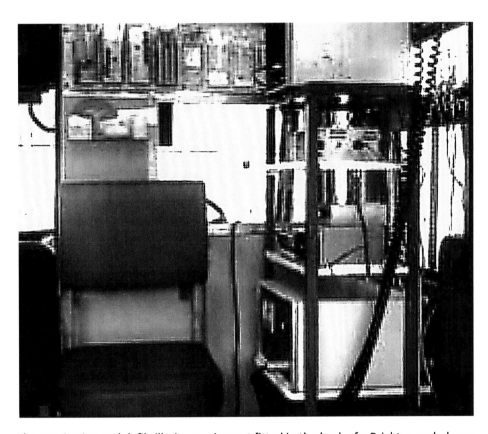

The monitoring and defibrillation equipment fitted in the back of a Brighton ambulance

The cardiac monitor and defibrillator were very heavy and had to be bolted onto a frame in the rear of the ambulance, consequently the patient had to be taken to the equipment rather than the other way round. When on standby at Brighton Ambulance Station the equipment was kept on mains charge otherwise it rapidly drained the vehicle's battery. The ambulance did not attend general 999 calls but was held back, along with its specially trained crew, for suspected cardiac emergencies. Its crew collected a doctor and nurse from Brighton Hospital en-route to the patient.

Extended 'Paramedic' Training

Dr. Douglas Chamberlain arrived in Brighton in 1970 to take up post as a consultant cardiologist at the Royal Sussex County **Hospital and** soon decided to set up a scheme to train Brighton ambulancemen to resuscitate patients from cardiac arrest without the intervention of a doctor.

Despite initial opposition from the medical establishment, ambulancemen, first from Brighton Ambulance Station and later from Hove, were taught the skills necessary to read an ECG and use a defibrillator, intubate patients and set up IV infusions. When they completed their training they became amongst the first ambulance staff in the country to be termed 'Paramedics'.

Professor Douglas Chamberlain OBE.

Burgess Hill Ambulance Station, 1970. The ambulances are, from left to right, an ex British Red Cross Bedford J Type and three East Sussex County Council Bedford J Types, the centre one with Hewson bodywork.

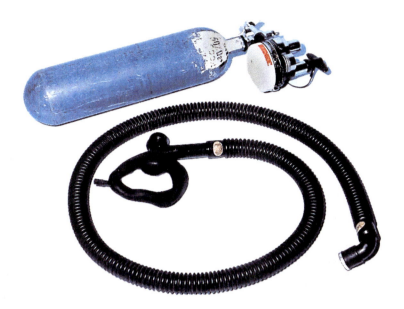

Entonox, an analgesic gas mixture of 50% Oxygen and 50% Nitrous Oxide, was first introduced into East Sussex Ambulance Service in 1969, followed a year later by the West Sussex Ambulance Service. Prior to its introduction ambulance staff had no means of administering any form of pain relief, the patients having to wait until they arrived at hospital before their pain could be treated.

A Bedford J Type and a Bedford CA ambulance, both with Lomas bodywork, at Hastings Ambulance Station in 1970.

An East Sussex County Council Lomas bodied Bedford J1 ambulance
arriving at a road traffic accident on Staplefield Common circa 1970.

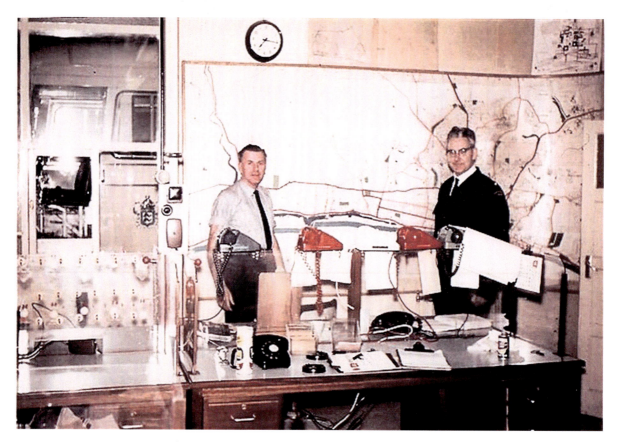

Brighton Borough Ambulance Service control room, 1971.

Control Assistant L/A Bob Foden and Station Officer Frank (Swoop) Hurley in the new control room in
Brighton Ambulance Station circa 1971. The Red phones are 999, Green ones go direct to the Fire
Station at Preston Circus and the Blue one is a direct line to the Police Station.

A 1970/1 Hewson bodied Bedford J1 and a 1967 registered Lomas bodied J1 at Hailsham Ambulance Station circa 1971.

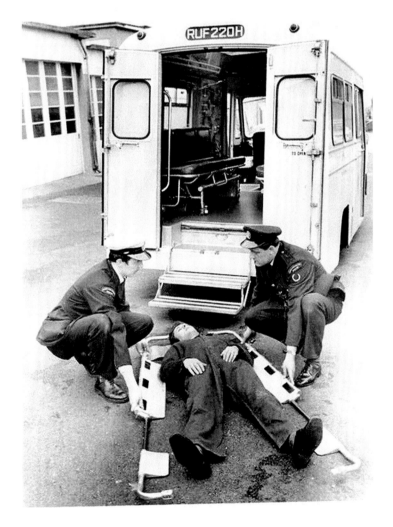

Brighton ambulancemen on the forecourt of Brighton Ambulance Station demonstrating the use of a two piece orthopaedic or 'scoop' stretcher in 1971.

Hastings Ambulance Service 1971

The agency agreement by which the St. John Ambulance Brigade operated the ambulance service for Hastings Borough Council came to an end at midnight on September 30th 1971, the staff transferring to the newly formed Hastings Ambulance Service which came into effect at 00.01 hours on the 1st of October.

Hastings Ambulance Service as an independent service itself only lasted for three years, coming to an end on March 31st 1974, when it was incorporated into the newly formed East Sussex Area Health Authority's service.

EAST SUSSEX WIN REGIONAL AMBULANCE CONTEST

Should you be unfortunate enough to be involved in an accident, you can rest assured that with the East Sussex Ambulance Service you will be in safe and competent hands. For it was East Sussex that gained overall highest marks in the No 5 Region ambulance efficiency contest arranged by the National Association of Ambulance Officers, at Bexhill, on Saturday.

Teams from Sussex, Surrey, Kent, Hertfordshire, Essex, Hampshire and London competed. The East Sussex team gained the Victor Ludorum Shield, presented by the Ford Motor Company, for winning the contest. In fact, two East Sussex pairs tied for it; Newhaven control officer Paul Stredwick and ambulanceman Paul Haynes, and ambulancemen Peter Wooller and Barry Tiller from Haywards Heath. They had to attend a mock collision between a car and a vehicle carrying acid. The object was that the men should appreciate the dangers involved, carry out all the right procedures, and protect themselves from the hazards, in addition to administering first aid.

The Wadham Cup for the winner of the Team Test went to the Hastings Ambulance Service pair of Andrew Parr and Francis Radford, with the Haywards Heath team of Peter Wooler and Barry Tiller being the runners-up, and taking the Lomas Shield. The Entonox Cup for the best attendant went to Andrew Parr of Hastings, with Paul Stredwick, of Newhaven, runner-up.

Hastings Borough Ambulance Service will now provide the attendant and team test pair to No5 Region in the finals at Stoke Mandeville on August 20th. All competitors were given souvenir medallions by the East Sussex County Council Health Committee.

WEST SUSSEX COUNTY HEALTH DEPARTMENT
AMBULANCE SERVICE

Ambulancemen

Vacancies at Bognor Regis, Pulborough, Chichester and Worthing. Candidates must live locally and be willing to be trained. Basic starting pay £18.50 p.w. (£19.72½ p.w. with current first-aid certificate) rising with appropriate experience and training to £20.07½ p.w. Uniform provided, standby allowances.

Ambulancewomen

Part-time vacancies at Horsham and Chichester. Duties involve conveyance of walking cases. Hours of duty 8.15 a.m. to 4.30 p.m. with one hour for lunch. (36¼ hour 5 day week). Uniform supplied. Candidates should live locally, be experienced drivers and have a knowledge of first-aid or willing to be trained. Basic salary £16.77 p.w. (more if first-aid certificate held).

Send postcard for details and application form to County Health Department, Metropolitan House, Northgate, Chichester.

Newspaper advert circa 1971/2

Extract from the Sussex Express, 30th June 1972.

Worthing Ambulance Station in 1972. The fleet includes two Mk1 Ford Transits, two BMC LDs and two BMC J2s, all with bodywork by Wadhams of Waterlooville.

Ambulances and fire appliances at a major incident exercise staged by West Sussex County Council in Chichester railway station goods yard, circa 1972.

Built on land immediately adjacent to Chichester Ambulance Station in Summersdale Road, West Sussex County Council opened this new purpose-designed County Ambulance Control Centre in 1973.

The last ambulance station to be built by West Sussex County Council was this one in Ifield Avenue Crawley. Opened in 1973 and built to a completely different design to the council's earlier ambulance stations, it replaced the town's old ambulance station in Exchange Road.

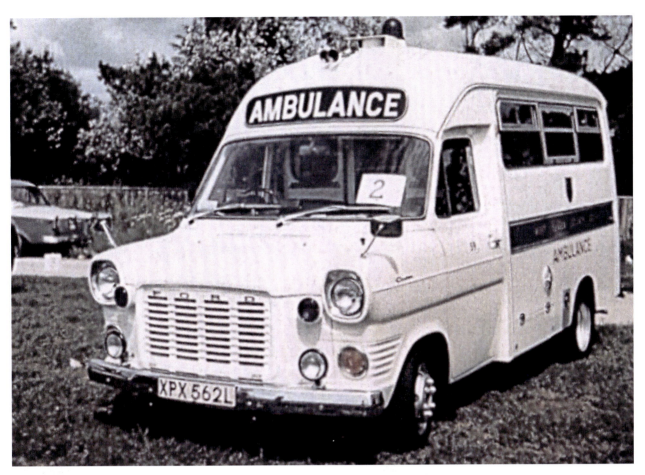

Bognor based Ford Transit ambulance, call sign 59, at West End Park, Bognor, awaiting the start of the town's 1973 carnival procession. Delivered new to the station in 1973, this Hanlon bodied example was the first of the new 3 litre V6 versions of the Mk1 Transit to be based in the town.

Delivered new to Hastings Ambulance Service in 1973, this Hanlon bodied
Bedford CF was fitted with two trolley-cots.

Staff at Bognor Regis Ambulance Station in 1973

L/R: Back row, Keith Merryman, Michael Airey, Dennis Croucher, Vince Shaw, Tim Murgatroyd, Roger Farley and Dennis Highfield. Front row, Roy Tharle, Brian Knight, Station Officer Peter Wells, Peggy Newman and Andy Brian.

No.5 Region Ambulance Competition (Winchester) 1973

Among the competitors taking part in the Regional Finals that year were teams from Hampshire, East and West Sussex, Surrey, Hampshire and Kent. The competition was staged at a school in Winchester, and among those in the East and West Sussex teams are Andy Parr, 'Tiny' Etherington, Collin Burden, Alan Shadbolt, Gerry Radford, Trevor Wiles, Tony Chapman, John Armes, Mike Hole and Nigel Miles,

Hayward Heath Red Cross Centre's 1972/3 registered BMC JU250 ambulance in 1973.

Hastings Borough Ambulance Service's Bedford J1 ambulances, a 1971/2 registered DXD 675J and 1969/70 registered HDY 470G, photographed at an ambulance efficiency competition circa 1974.

The Area Health Authority Services, 1974–1982

Two events were to change the organisation of Sussex's ambulance services in the mid 1970s.

The first was the report by the Commission on Local Government that re-drew the boundary line between East and West Sussex. The second was the implementation of the National Health Service Reorganisation Act of 1973, which transferred the responsibility for the provision of an ambulance service from the county and borough councils to the National Health Service.

The new West Sussex Area Health Authority Ambulance Service took over the ambulance service from the West Sussex County Council on April 1st, 1974. As a result of the county boundary changes the towns of East Grinstead, Haywards Heath and Burgess Hill, previously in East Sussex, became part of West Sussex, and their ambulance staff and ambulance stations were transferred to the new West Sussex Area Health Authority Ambulance Service, which had its new headquarters in the West Sussex Area Health Authority building at Courtlands, Worthing. Mr. Pat Weeks was appointed as its first Chief Ambulance Officer.

In East Sussex, the three Borough services of Brighton, Hastings and Eastbourne, along with the East Sussex County Council run service that covered the remaining areas of the county, were incorporated into the new East Sussex Area Health Authority Ambulance Service on April 1st 1974 with its headquarters in Eastbourne, and Mr. Rowland Granger was appointed as the services Chief Ambulance Officer.

Crawley Ambulance Staff in 1974

Back row L/R: John Cornell, Douglas Hallam, Dick Woods, Fergie Nottman, Ron Durrant, John Berry, John Pawsey, Brian Kelly, Ted Hillier, Chris Morehead, Peter Tidy.
Front row L/R: Pete Riley, Jack Pitts, Roger Saych, Station Officer Len Riley, Goff Tame, Derek Hill, Cecil Tuckey.

Two of the first extended trained Hove ambulancemen, Dereck Emery and Mike 'Tiny' Etherington, with Hove's first cardiac equipped ambulance, a Bedford CF, circa 1974.

SPN 375G, a 1968/9 registered Newhaven based East Sussex County Council Ambulance Service Bedford J1 on Brighton seafront in the mid 1970's, being closely followed by an E-Type Jaguar.

1965 registered Bedford J1 ambulance DAP 161C at the old Hailsham St John's ambulance station in Groveland Road, circa 1974. Initially an East Sussex County Council vehicle, it has had the County Council's crest removed and now simply displays "East Sussex Area Health Authority Ambulance Service" lettering along its side. This style of lettering appeared on county council ambulances for a short period after the service became a part of the NHS in 1974.

An East Sussex AHA Ambulance Service Austin 3 Litre ambulance at Hastings Ambulance Station circa late 1974. Originally delivered new to the old Hastings Ambulance Service, this Wadham Stringer conversion was fitted with a single stretcher and used for long distance journeys.

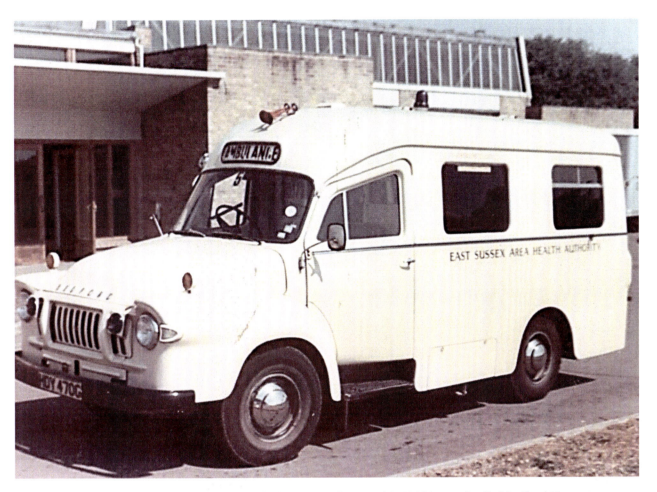

Hastings Ambulance Station in the later part of 1974. This 1969 Lomas bodied Bedford J1
HDY 470G was originally part of the Hastings Ambulance Service fleet before being
transferred to the East Sussex Area Health Authority Ambulances Service.

The rear saloon of HDY 470G, the same Bedford J1 as in above photo,
showing the Lomas Low-Loading stretcher system.

East Sussex staff moving patients out when Eastbourne's Gildredge Hospital closed in 1974.

A Wadham bodied BMC JU250 SCV outside the main entrance to Eastbourne General Hospital in 1974.

East Sussex Area Health Authority's 1974/5 registered Bedford CF with bodywork by
Wadhams of Waterlooville.

Newhaven based Bedford J1 ambulance at the scene of a devastating fire at Arrow Tyres, Newhaven, on 19th July
1976. A total of four ambulances attended the scene during the day to treat those injured in the incident, and at
least one ambulance was present late into the night

Staff at the East Sussex Ambulance Control in Southview Road, Eastbourne in the mid 1970s.

WAP 298P, a newly delivered Wadham bodied Bedford CF front line ambulance at Eastbourne Ambulance Station in 1976.

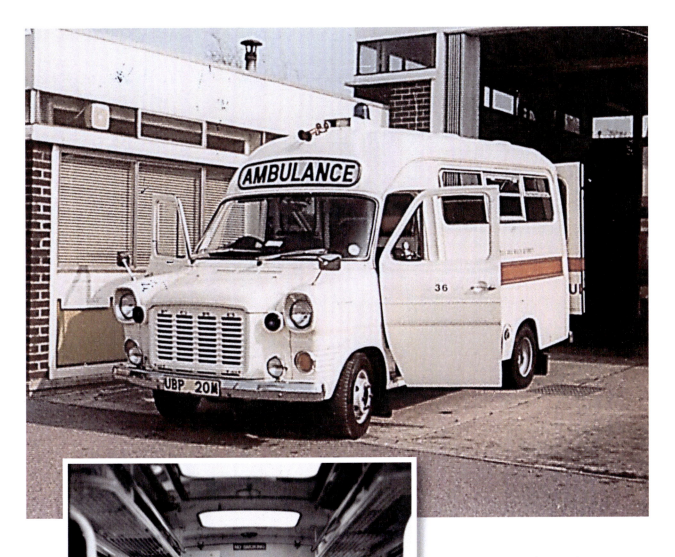

Above: Bognor's 1973/4 registered 3 litre V6 Hanlon bodied Mk1 Ford Transit on the station forecourt in 1976.

Left: The typical internal layout of a Hanlon Bodied Ford Transit of the type shown in the photograph above. On the left is a non-elevating York 2 trolley-cot with an elevating York 4 on the right. Equipment stowage was in the over- cab and n/s front lockers, with blankets usually stowed on the high mounted side racks.

East Sussex staff taking part in the 1977 Eastbourne Carnival.

Back row (left to right)
Arthur Dunmall, Brian Field, Alan Shadbolt, Mel Needham.

Front row
Trevor Pierce, Barry Muir, Keith Marshal, Peter Kenney and Tony Essam (on the stretcher).

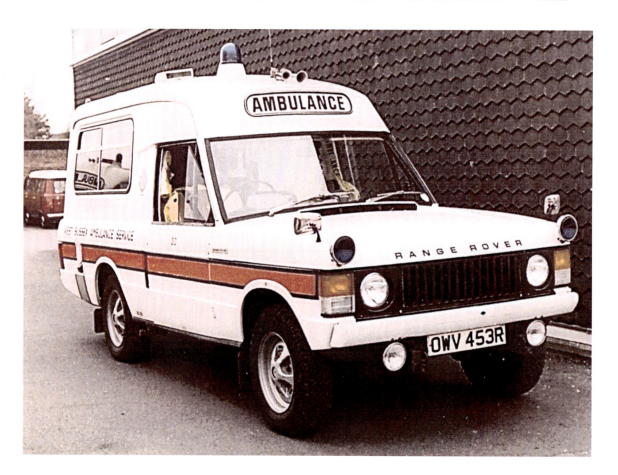

Worthing based Lomas bodied Range Rover in 1977. These vehicles replaced the old Series 2 Land Rovers, which were then used as incident support units.

KBP 594J, a 1970/71 registered Wadham bodied Mk1 Ford Transit parked on the forecourt of Chichester Ambulance Station in 1977. This ex West Sussex County Council Ambulance Service vehicle still carries the County Council crest but has had its original blue side-stripes replaced with high-vis orange ones.

Crawley based 1972/3 registered Hanlon bodied 3 litre Mk1 Ford Transit
ambulance XPX 565L, call-sign 64, photographed circa 1977/8.

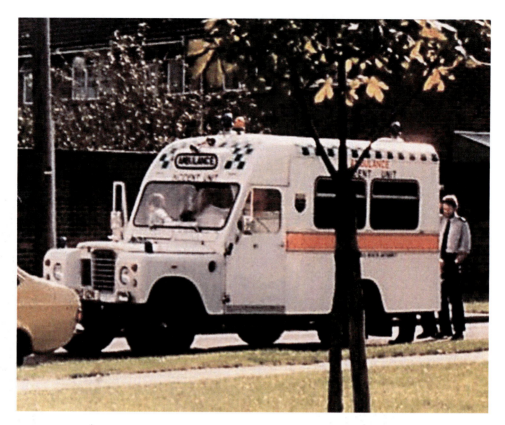

This is an old ex-West Sussex County Council service Series 2 Land Rover photographed in 1978. Based in Crawley, and still carrying the County Council crest, it was by then in use as an Incident Support Unit.

The staff at Bognor Regis ambulance station in 1979.

Back row L/R: Paul Pope, Dennis Highfield, Fred Botterill, Jim Phillips, Dennis Chroucher, Allan Benson, Peggy Newman, Vince Shaw, Barry Welsh, Adrian White, Tim Murgatroyd, Andy Brian.
Front row L/R: Station Officer Brian Knight, John Richards, Brian Janman, Roy Tharle, Gil Lumsden, Mick Airey, Phil Cooke.

The staff at Hove Ambulance Station in 1980.

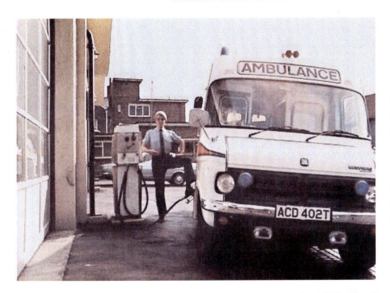

Ken Walter refuelling a Bedford
CF ambulance at Eastbourne
Ambulance Station in 1980.
A number of other ambulance
stations had fuel on site, including
Haywards Heath, Burgess Hill,
East Grinstead, Chichester, Hove,
Newhaven and Brighton.

Staff from Pulborough Ambulance
Station were able to equip all three of
the station's vehicles with defibrillators,
cardiac monitoring and advanced airway
management equipment after setting up
the charity 'Arun Cardiac Emergency'
(ACE) in 1978 with the support of local
GP Dr Shillingford (lying on the stretcher
in this photo from 1981).
Following the success of this scheme,
other stations across the county set up
similar charities of their own.

Control staff raising a toast at the opening of the newly refitted mobilization bay in the West Sussex Ambulance Control Centre in Summersdale Road, Chichester in 1981

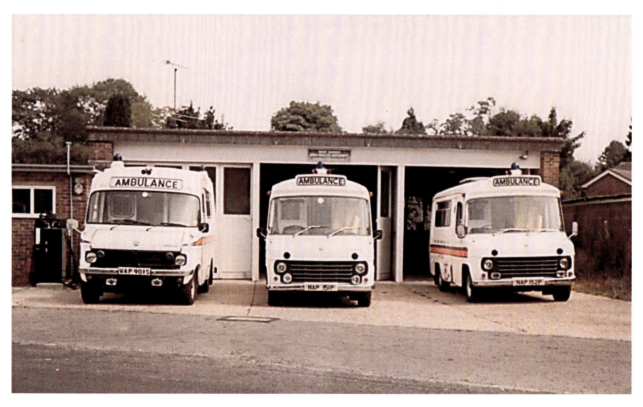

One Hanlon bodied Bedford CF ambulance and two Wadham bodied versions on the forecourt of Haywards Heath Ambulance Station in Bridge Road circa 1981.

1982 – East & West Sussex Ambulance Services

The consultative paper 'Patients First' issued by the Secretary of State for Social Services in 1979 paved the way for the next major change in the way that health services were provided nationally.

Its aim was to eliminate one layer of administration, the Area Health Authorities, and devolve the provision of health services down to district level. The 1980 Health Services Bill came into effect on April 1st 1982, and, in West Sussex, with the abolition of the old Area Health Authority, the Chichester, Worthing and Mid Downs District Health Authorities took charge of their own affairs.

Because the ambulance service was a 'county wide' organisation that would be difficult and un-economic to split into three separate services, Worthing District Health Authority undertook the management of the service on behalf of the other West Sussex districts, with all three authorities contributing their own share of the services budget. This new service was renamed the West Sussex Ambulance Service.

In East Sussex the same happened, with each health district contributing their share of the budget to the newly named East Sussex Ambulance Service, which had its headquarters in the grounds of Eastbourne General Hospital.

Unable to obtain new vehicles quickly enough from their usual ambulance builders, East Sussex Ambulance Service tagged an order for a number of these Dormobile bodied Bedford CF ambulances onto a batch ordered by the London Ambulance Service. This is SWV 768R at Bexhill Ambulance Station circa 1983.

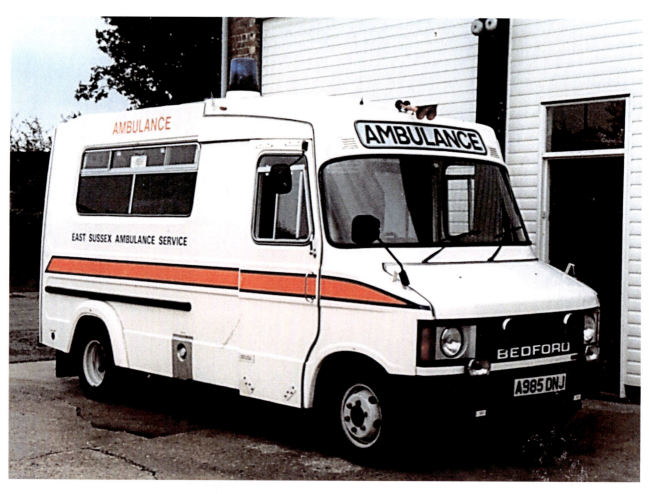

East Sussex Ambulance Service's 1983 registered Hanlon bodied Bedford CF, A985 DNJ, at Hailsham Ambulance Station.

Crawley based sitting case vehicle ENJ 989V, a 1979/80 registered Hanlon bodied
Bedford CF, call-sign 127, at Crawley Hospital in 1983.

Chichester Ambulance Station entered teams into the Royal Military Police March for several years. This is the 1983 team ready for the parade through Chichester city centre after completing a 40km walk over the South Downs.

Heathfield Ambulance Station in Burwash Road in1983 with a number of Bedford CF front-line ambulances and sitting case vehicles parked out in the sunshine.

A 1981/2 registered East Sussex Ambulance Service, Hanlon bodied, long wheelbase Bedford CF
on the forecourt of Newhaven Ambulance Station in 1983.

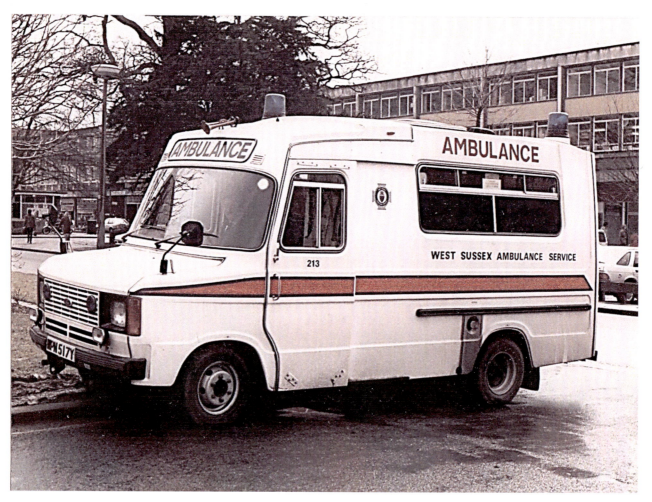

Crawley's 1982/3 registered Hanlon bodied Mk2 Ford Transit call-sign Chicam 213, at Crawley Hospital in 1983.

This Ford Granada was nicknamed 'The Hearse' – because that's what it was originally built to be – it was used as a driver training vehicle. It was very quick but didn't handle so well, and gave many driving course participants moments to remember while on high speed training runs.

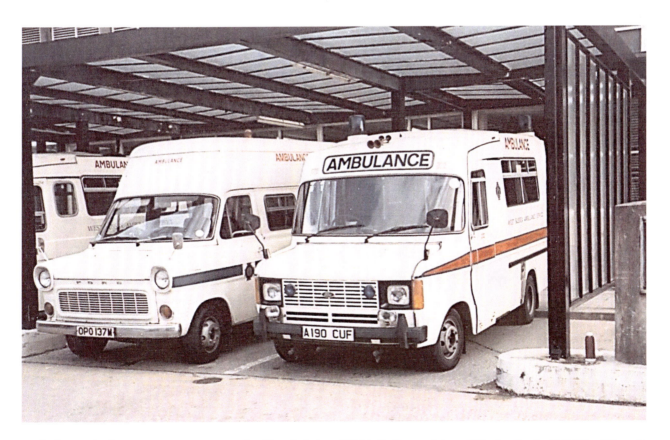

Parked outside the main entrance to Crawley Hospital circa 1984 is Pulborough based Hanlon bodied Mk2 Ford Transit A190 CUF, call-sign 02. Alongside it, and still in the old West Sussex County Council's cream and blue livery, is OPO 137M, Horsham Ambulance Station's 1974/5 registered Mk1 Transit sitting case vehicle, call-sign Chicam 39.

Ambulanceman Phil McGovern manning a display stand at the Bognor Lions Club carnival in West Park in August 1984. Alongside Bognor's brand new Hanlon High-line bodied Mk2 Ford Transit ambulance there is a display of resuscitation and training equipment. Proceeds from the carnival went towards the purchase of Bognor Ambulance Station's first defibrillator.

Burgess Hill ambulance and fire stations were built alongside each other, and held a joint open day in 1984.

Kenny Walters at the dispatch desk in the East Sussex Ambulance Service control room in 1984. The control was located within the services HQ complex which consisted of a number of inter-linked portable buildings in the grounds of Eastbourne District General Hospital.

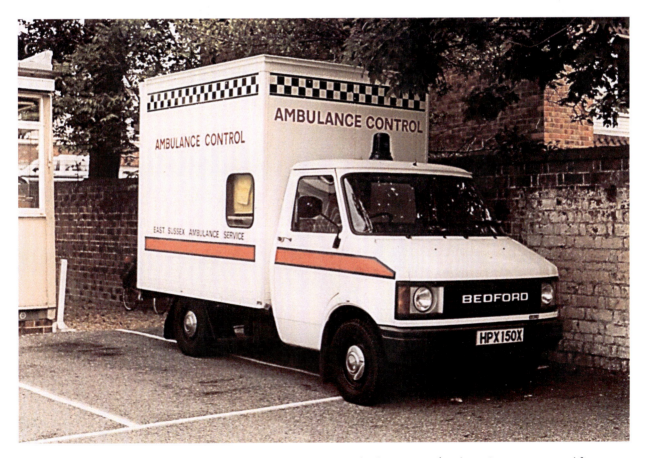

East Sussex Ambulance Service's mobile control unit, photographed circa 1984/5. The unit was converted from a mobile audiology unit on a 1981/2 registered Bedford CF chassis.

Crowborough staff at the Eastbourne 999 Show in the mid-1980's.

L/R John Clifton, Guy Emery, Steve Woods, Dave Keeley and Simon Fermer.

Eastbourne Station Officer Ken Hilton circa 1985.

The new Crown Badge was given the royal seal of approval by Her Majesty Queen Elizabeth II and dedicated to the National Health Service Ambulance Services of England and Wales at a service held at York Minster on September the 19th 1985.

East Sussex Ambulance Service's 1982/3 registered Hanlon bodied Bedford CF ambulance parked outside the Brompton Hospital, Fulham Road, London, in 1986. It is displaying the newly issued Crown Badge.

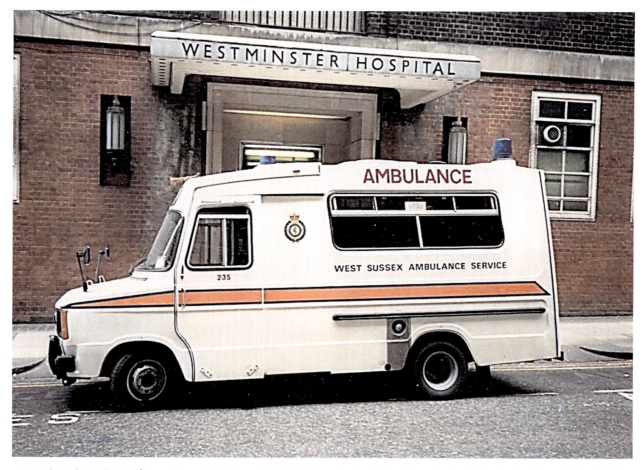

Worthing based 1983/4 registered Mk2 Transit A191 CUF, call-sign 235, at London's Westminster Hospital in 1986.

East Sussex Ambulance Service took delivery of this Volkswagen LT 31 ambulance with its futuristic looking coachwork by Taurus Bodies of Stockport, Cheshire, in 1986. It quickly gained the nickname 'Thunderbird 4'.

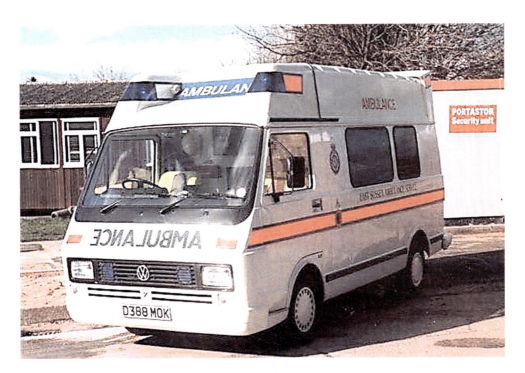

D388 MOK photographed at Hailsham Ambulance Station later in 1986 with its livery changed to the services standard orange side stipes. The vehicle did the rounds of East Sussex Ambulance Stations for service trials, and went on display at the 1986 Eastbourne 999 show. The type proved less than popular with road staff as it had a very heavy clutch, no power steering and a poor turning circle.

ECD 983V, a 1979/80 registered Bedford CF, at Eastbourne General Hospital in 1986. Initially a front line vehicle, it has had the lower half of its bodywork painted green, denoting that it has been re-allocated to the services second tier PTS fleet.

Chichester based Ford Transit sitting case vehicle D748 GBP, call-sign 191,
at Shoreham Ambulance Station circa 1987.

Chichester Red Cross Centre's 1982 registered Ford Transit ambulance in North Street, Chichester,
during the city's 1987 carnival procession.

Bognor Regis St John Ambulance Division's 1976 Wadhams bodied Bedford CF in West Park, Bognor, waiting for the start of the town's 1987 carnival parade. It was an ex West Sussex Ambulance Service vehicle previously based at Burgess Hill.

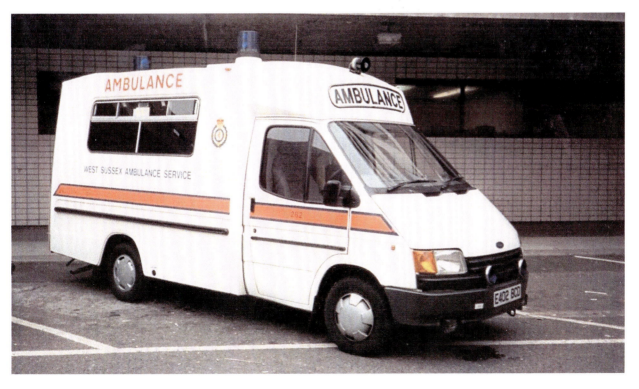

The new shape Mk3 Ford Transit was soon adopted by ambulance manufacturers and by 1987 the first of the Hanlon bodied versions was in service in West Sussex. Photographed at Southampton General Hospital in 1987, E402 BCD, call-sign 282 was based in Worthing.

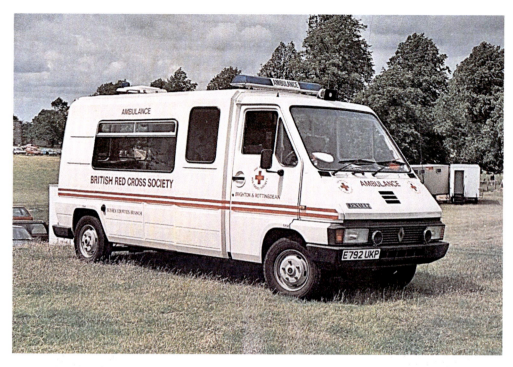

Brighton & Hove Red Cross Centre's Renault Master ambulance in 1987.

A brand new a 1987/8 registered long wheelbase Hanlon bodied Bedford CF, E730 HXC, at Crowborough Ambulance Station circa 1988. These vehicles were fitted with a 3.3 litre straight six Holden engine and had a fuel consumption of a mere 18mpg. The vehicle carries the newly introduced small green and white chequered side stripes.

This 1978 Ford A Series vehicle was initially a PTS vehicle based at Bognor Regis. It was fitted with a powered lift at the rear and carried a crew of two, and with the fleet number 321 it soon gained the nickname 'Dusty Bin' after a character on a popular TV quiz show of the period. It was found to be unsuitable for the PTS role and within a few years it had been taken over by ambulance control staff in Chichester who converted it into a mobile control unit. In this 1988 photo it is parked at the rear of Ambulance Control in Summersdale Road, Chichester.

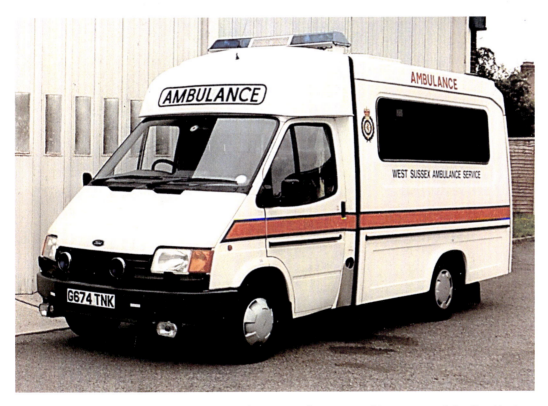

Littlehampton's 1989 registered Mk 3 Ford Transit, call-sign 242. This was one of the first Hanlon M.I.A.B. bodied (Modular Interchangeable Ambulance Body) vehicles to enter service in West Sussex. M.I.A.B. bodywork was constructed and mounted in such a way that it could be taken off a chassis that had reached the end of it life and be re-mounted on a new one.

Staff on the picket line outside Burgess Hill Ambulance Station during the 1989/90 National Ambulance Dispute.

Brighton staff on Brighton seafront during the 1989/90 National Ambulance Dispute.

West Sussex officers at Worthing District Health Authorities headquarters at Courtlands, Worthing, In June 1990.

L/R back row: Bert Manning, Norman Oakley, Derek Hill, Brian Knight, Brian Attfield, Peter Tidy and David Rice.
L/R front row: Peter Wells, Peter Williams, Allan Ware, Chief Ambulance Officer Ken Smith, David Hook, Bob Jeffries, John Layhe, Dennis Tennent, Jim Boxhall.

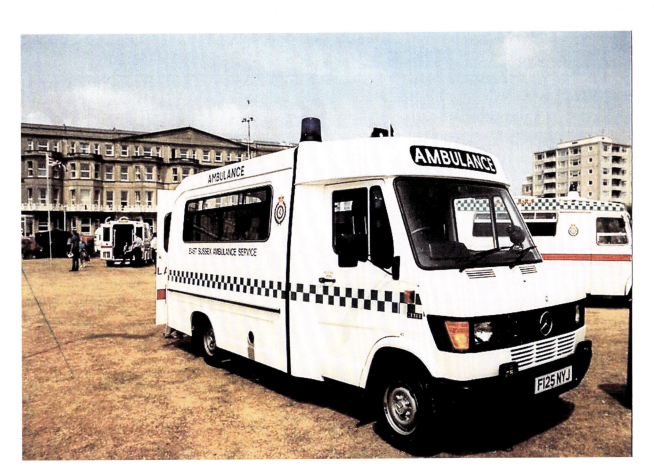

Crowborough based F125 NYJ, a 1989 registered Mercedes 310 ambulance with Wadhams Pioneer M.I.A.B. body work, on display at the 1990 Eastbourne 999 show.

West Sussex purchased this dual purpose vehicle in 1990. A Customline bodied LDV, it was fitted for driver training and as a mobile control unit. There was seating in the front for up to four students plus the driving instructor and a door in the cab led through into a fully equipped incident control office in the rear compartment.

Hastings based Mercedes 310 at the Conquest Hospital circa 1990.

Following a period of fund-raising, three West Sussex ambulancemen and women, along with a nurse from Worthing, undertook a long overland journey to Timisoara in Romania in November 1990. Their aim was to deliver two decommissioned West Sussex ambulances, both full of medical supplies and humanitarian aid, to the town's hospital. L/R: Neil Monery, Nurse Sue Flin, Helen Davey and Chris Williams at Chichester Ambulance Station prior to setting off on their journey

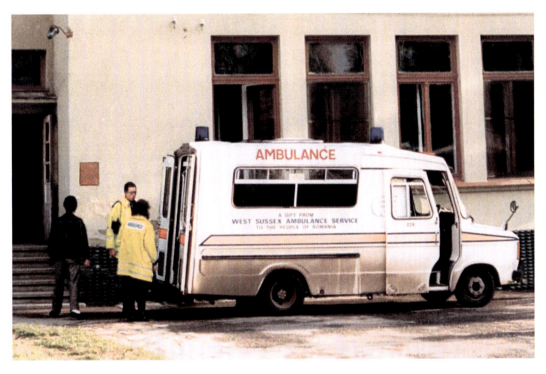

Unloading one of the ambulances at Timisoara Hospital.

Hailsham staff with the stations first defibrillator, donated to the service by the Charles Hunt Day Centre circa 1991. Kneeling in front are Bob Morris and Joe Garcia, the first two from Hailsham to qualify as paramedics. Standing behind them are Bob Catt, George Bodimede, Mick Holmes, Jim Morgan, Mick Hill and Reg Gates. On the far right is Divisional Officer Doug Maine.

East Sussex Ambulance Service's 1990/1 registered Renault 21 officer's car at Brighton Ambulance Station circa 1991.

Ever since the introduction of a two-tier service in 1987, West Sussex Ambulance Service's Patient Transport Service staff had been using spare front line ambulances for their work. In 1991 the service introduced a fleet of dedicated second tier PTS vehicles based on the Renault Master chassis. One of them, H883 EKE, is shown here at Bognor Ambulance Station in May 1991. These vehicles were capable of carrying both sitting case and stretcher patients, and importantly for the crews working them, they had a much lower loading height than the existing front line ambulances.

Ambulancemen to take to the skies

Ambulancemen in West Sussex are taking to the air on their missions of mercy.

West Sussex Chief Ambulance Officer Ken Smith said in his annual report that in conjunction with East Sussex the service was carrying out a pilot study in the use of helicopters.

They were co-operating with Sussex police in putting a paramedic on the police helicopter.

"This gives us better coverage than we otherwise would have, and the project will be evaluated over an 18 month period to assess its future potential." said Mr Smith.

from the *West Sussex Gazette* July 6th 1991

WEST SUSSEX AMBULANCE SERVICE

Patient Transport Service

Driving a West Sussex Ambulance means having a real and valued job within the Community, getting people to hospitals for out-patient appointments, regular treatment or day hospital care.

If you are good driver with a current licence, between 18 and 55 and physically fit, we would like to hear from you.

We are currently seeking full-time and part-time staff. If you are looking for an interesting and rewarding job, where training is provided, and have held a clean current driving licence for at least one year and would like to know more, please come along to:
Crawley Ambulance Station, Ifield Road, Crawley, between 09.00 hours and 18.00 on Wednesday 21st August, 1991.

West Sussex County Times August 16th 1991

The students on West Sussex Ambulance Service's first 'in-house' Paramedic Extended Training Course at Swandean Hospital in 1991.

L/R: Larry Walker from Worthing, Roy Nightingale – East Grinstead, Julian Fagg – Haywards Heath, Clive Ewing – Chichester, Phil Hammerton – Shoreham, Bob Higgs – Bognor and Peter Purdew – Horsham. The three instructors are L/R: Bert Manning, Dereck Hill and Antell McDonald.

East Sussex Ambulance Service Special Operations Response Team, aka 'The Riot Mob', circa 1992.

Back row L/R: Steve Pannett, Geoff Gander, Clive Butler, John Stewart, Mick Hill, Neil Taylor. Front row L/R: Tim Fellows, Dougie Mayne, Joe Garcia, Rob Jones, Bob Earl.

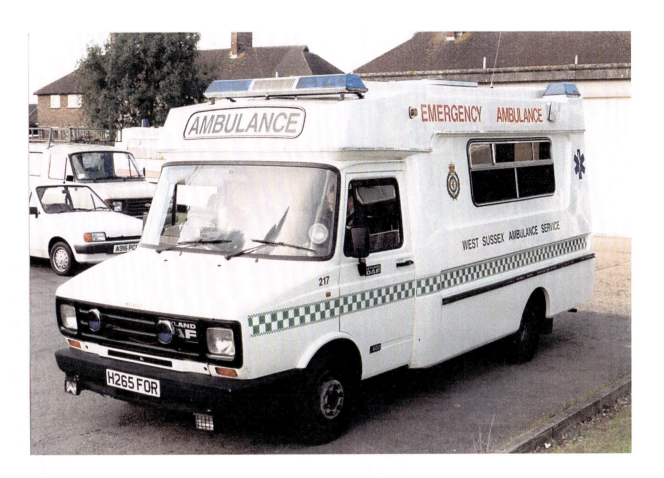

217, West Sussex Ambulance Service's Mountain Range bodied Leyland-Daf in 1992. This diesel engined vehicle was briefly based at Burgess Hill before it was transferred to Worthing and used as a long distance PTS vehicle.

Worthing St. John and Red Cross units during a joint major incident exercise with West Sussex Ambulance Service at the disused Shoreham Cement Works In 1992.

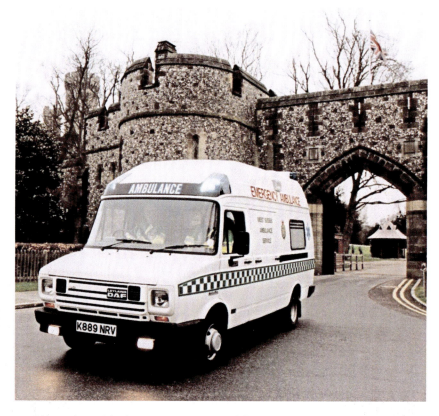

Pictured outside the entrance to Arundel Castle in December 1992, this publicity photo features K889 NRV, a 1992 registered Customline bodied Leyland Daf, one of the new fleet of ambulances introduced that year. This vehicle went on to be based at Crawley with the call sign G189.

Photographed at an overnight stop in Donja Brela, Croatia, are Andy Brian, Jo Panchen and Brian Janman, three of the six West Sussex ambulancemen and women who took part in 'Operation Angel', a humanitarian aid convoy to the former Yugoslavia in December 1993. The other three members of the team were Jim Vincent, Bert Greenfield and Gordon Bushell.

East Sussex Ambulance Service Renault Master ambulances circa 1993.

Worthing's new ambulance station in Yeoman Road, circa 1993. The station had been officially opened in September 1990 by Dr Douglas Chamberlain, Consultant Cardiologist at the Royal Sussex County Hospital.

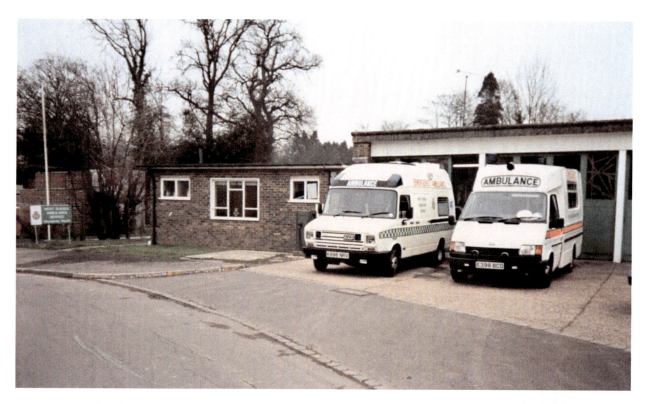

A Customline bodied Leyland Daf and a 1987/8 registered Hanlon bodied Ford Transit at Haywards Heath Ambulance Station in February 1993.

Homefield Park, Worthing, March 1993. A crew move a patient from their Leyland Daf Customline bodied ambulance into the London Air Ambulance for transfer to a specialist hospital. The aircraft, an AS365 Dauphin, registration G-HEMS, is in the orange livery of its sponsor, the Express Newspaper Group.

This Ford Mondeo Paramedic Rapid Response Vehicle, the first to enter service in the county, was bought as a result of intensive fund raising efforts by staff at Littlehampton Ambulance Station. Costing around £25,000 to buy and fully equip, it was handed over to West Sussex Chief Ambulance Officer Ken Smith by Paramedic Ron Patching at New England College, Arundel, in August 1993.

Pilots, Police Observers and Paramedics from both East and West Sussex Ambulance Services with the Sussex Police Air Support Unit Helicopter, A Bolkow BO105 Call sign 'Hotel 900' at its base at Shoreham Airport in 1994.

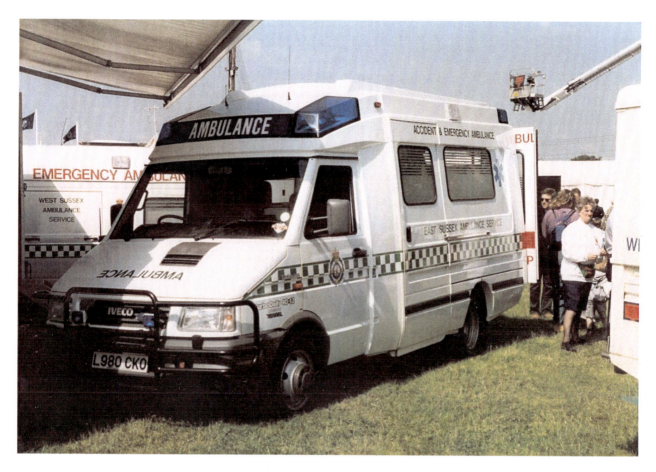

East Sussex Ambulance Service's Customline bodied Iveco Daily on the joint East and West Sussex Ambulance Service stand at the 1994 South of England Show, Ardingly.

East Sussex Ambulance Service's control room in Eastbourne in 1995.

Sussex Ambulance Service Trust 1995 – 2006

West Sussex Ambulance Service submitted an application for Trust Status to the Secretary of State for Health in 1993. Its stated aims were: *'To ensure that the West Sussex Ambulance Service NHS Trust will remain at the forefront of the provision of pre-hospital patient care and health transport services, and to build on the work of recent years to ensure that we continue to provide high quality, accessible services responsive to the particular needs of the population of West Sussex... As an NHS Trust, West Sussex Ambulance Service would remain an integral part of the National Health Service, but will benefit from a number of freedoms not available to a Directly Managed Unit.'*

An extract from the Services Trust application document 'Raising the Standards' goes on to say: *'That the Trust's Steering Group believe that an efficient and responsible management structure will lead to a better run ambulance service, allowing patients a greater say in the way in which they are treated',* and *'Increased operational independence will allow West Sussex Ambulance Service not only to meet the specified requirements of purchasers and staff, but to improve the quality of service to patients, taking account of their individual needs'.*

The service's application, along with the parallel application made by the East Sussex Ambulance Service, were turned down by the Secretary of State, who considered that a single ambulance trust covering the whole of Sussex would be more appropriate. Consequently a joint application was put forward for consideration and subsequently approved by the Secretary of State. The new **Sussex Ambulance Service NHS Trust** came into being on April 1st 1995, with its headquarters at 40-42 Fryers Walk, Lewes.

This service covered the counties of East and West Sussex from its new headquarters in Lewes until, along with both the Surrey and Kent services, it lost its individual county identity when it was amalgamated into the **South East Coast Ambulance Service NHS Trust** on July 1st 2006.

The Sussex Ambulance Service Trust moved into its new headquarters at 40-42 Friars Walk in Lewes in April 1995, but it was not until February 1997 that the two old county controls, previously in Eastbourne and Chichester, were combined in the new building.

The headquarters were officially opened by Baroness Jay, Minister of Health, on 28th November 1997.

David Griffiths, the first Chief Executive Officer of the new Sussex Ambulance Service Trust.

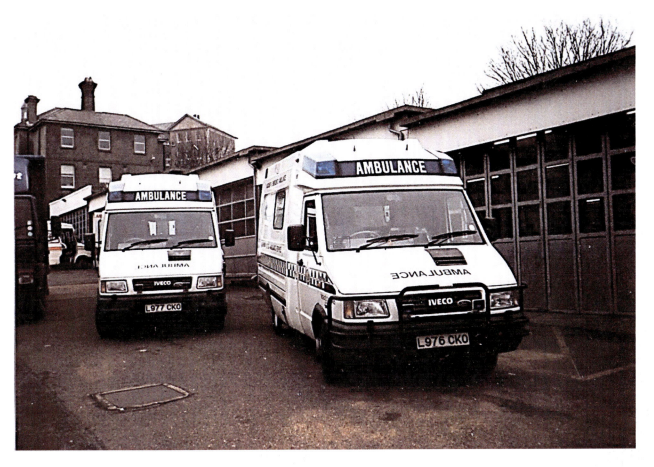

Two 1993/4 registered Iveco Turbo Daily ambulances with Customline Lazer bodywork
at Brighton Ambulance Station in 1995.

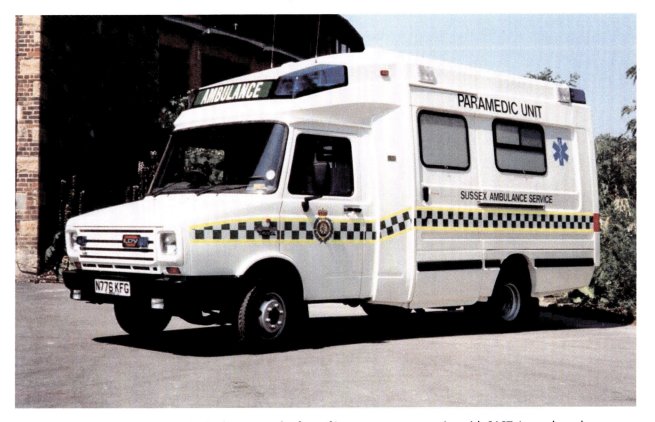

This Customline Lazer bodied LDV was the first of its type to enter service with SAST. It was based
in Newhaven and was donated to the service in 1996 by a Newhaven resident who gave it the
name 'Eric' in memory of her late brother.

Crawley based 1990/1 registered Renault Master Patient Transport Service vehicle, call sign G235, in March 1996.

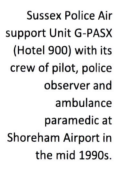
Sussex Police Air support Unit G-PASX (Hotel 900) with its crew of pilot, police observer and ambulance paramedic at Shoreham Airport in the mid 1990s.

Uckfield St John Ambulance Division's new Land Rover Defender ambulance in 1995.

Crawley based D429 YCD, a 1986 registered Land Rover Defender, fleet number G364, in June 1996. An ex West Sussex Ambulance Service unit, it now displays Sussex Ambulance Service livery.

The first three Sussex Ambulance Service paramedics to complete their heavy motorcycle course and to qualify as motorcycle responders in 1996 were Steve Connell, Graham Lelliot and Nick Baird. The course was run by PC Shaun Griffin from the Sussex Police headquarters in Lewes.

Sussex Ambulance Service officers, staff and trust directors with Baroness Cumberlidge at the 1996 SAST Annual Awards Ceremony held at Christs Hospital, Horsham on September 28th.

Presentation of an AED to the crew of Hotel 900 by Tony Smith (centre), the President of the East Brighton Rotary Club, on October 2nd 1996. L/R; Mick Evans, Keith Mitchell, Ken Smith, Andy Cashman and Nick Baird.

Wadham Stringer M.I.A.B. bodied Mercedes Benz 310, formally an East Sussex Ambulance Service vehicle, now displaying Sussex Ambulance Service markings in Hastings in 1997.

New Wheeled Coach bodied Chevrolet ambulances at the press launch at Michelham Priory in April 1997.

Customline Lazer bodied LDV at the Princess Royal Hospital in Haywards Heath in 1997.

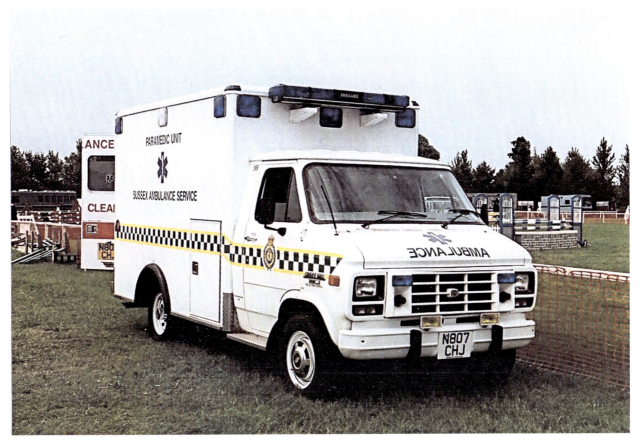

A Sussex Ambulance Service Wheeled Coach bodied Chevrolet ambulance photographed at a gymkhana 'somewhere in Sussex' in 1997. These Chevrolets were very heavily built and not terribly well liked by the crews. One big flaw on these vehicles, which had been converted from left hand drive, was the very tight driving cab and the lack of space in the driver's foot well. Other problems with them were their width, which made them difficult to manoeuvre in narrow streets, and their relatively poor brakes.

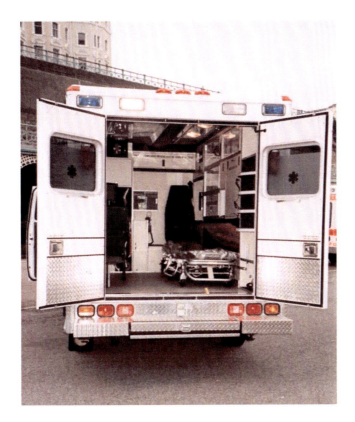

Interior view of the Chevrolet's rear saloon.

Press launch of the New Renault and Toyota PTS vehicles at Drucillas Park in November 1997.

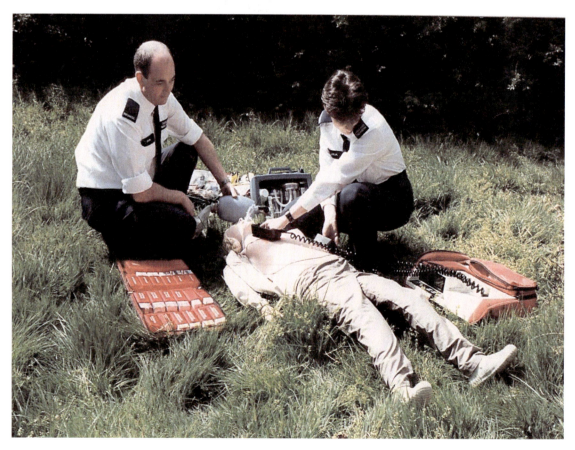

Resuscitation training with a Lifepak 10 cardiac monitor/defibrillator in 1997.

Bognor Regis Ambulance Station, August 1997

Taken on the day the station held its 'pre-demolition' staff party. The five ambulance lined up on the forecourt are two emergency ambulances, K882 NRV (Bravo 188) and N425 LPN (Lazer bodied Bravo 129) along with three PTS vehicles; a brand new double crewed outpatient transport Renault, an urgent case vehicle and a Ford Transit sitting case vehicle.

These three gentlemen were all honoured guests at Bognor Ambulance Station's 'pre-demolition' party.

All three were, at one time or another, Chief Ambulance Officers in the West Sussex Ambulance Service. On the left is Vince Glover, CAO 1963-1975, centre is Pat Weeks, CAO 1974-1989, and on the right is Ken Smith, CAO 1989 to 1996.

Dr Priscilla Mathew-Noble with Sussex Police Air Support Unit's Bolkow 109 helicopter G-PASX (Hotel 900) at Shoreham Airport circa late 1990's. She was a GP in Steyning and a founder member of SIMCAS, the Sussex & Surrey Immediate Care Scheme, and occasionally flew as a volunteer doctor on the helicopter.

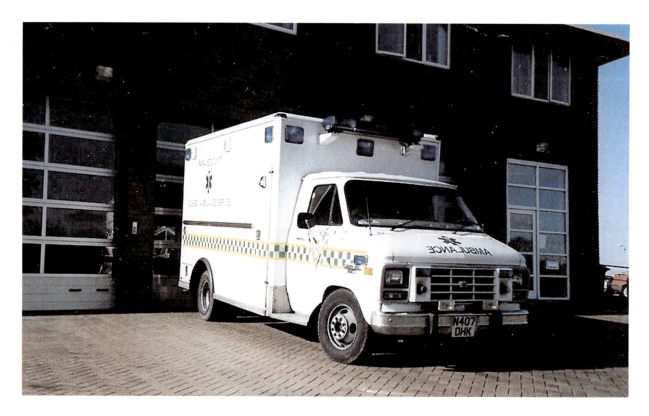

One of the new Chevrolet ambulances at Uckfield Ambulance Station in 1997.

CEO David Griffiths and Baroness Jay, Minister for Health, at the official opening ceremony for SAST's new headquarters in Friars Walk, Lewes, Friday 28th November 1997.

Signing the Sussex Ambulance Reserve Agreement on April 15th 1998 were, on behalf of the Sussex Ambulance Service, Chief Executive David Griffith, Anthony de Sautoy, Director of the Sussex Branch of the British Red Cross Society and Rosalind Stenning, Deputy Commissioner for St. John Ambulance Sussex. The agreement, drawn up by Andy Parr, Sussex Ambulance Service's Emergency Planning Manager, marked the formal inauguration of the Sussex Ambulance Service Reserve, intended to assist and support the service in time of need.

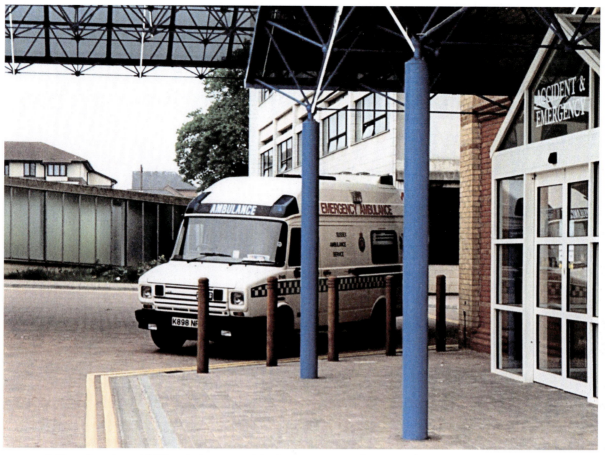

A Shoreham based LDV ambulance outside the entrance to the new A/E Department at Worthing Hospital in 1998. Note how just the word 'West' has been removed from the county title, leaving just a rather wonky 'Sussex Ambulance Service'.

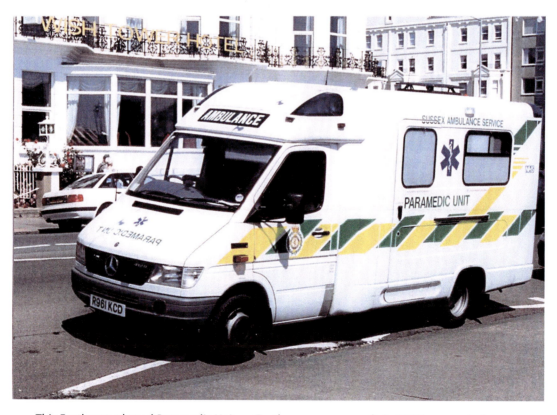

This Eastbourne based Paramedic Unit on Eastbourne promenade in 1998 was part of a new fleet of Mercedes 412D ambulances introduced to the county during 1997/8. It has UVG Premia style bodywork and displays the short lived diagonal livery.

Sussex Ambulance Service Colour party at the 1998 Annual Awards
Ceremony held at Slaugham Manor, near Haywards Heath.
L/R: Douglas Mayne, Andy Moyes, Jon Steele, and Dee D'Costa.

Work began on SAST's new central Fleet Maintenance Centre in Southdowns Road, Lewes, in September 1998, and
it was in use the next year. This photograph shows the interior of the workshop in 1999 with mechanics working or
a Toyota 4x4 and a Mercedes Sprinter ambulance.

Two views of a new UVG Premia bodied Renault Master PTS unit in the car park at the rear of SAST's HQ in Friars Walk, Lewes in January 1999. Of interest is the stretcher mounted transversely immediately behind the drivers cab.

A Toyota 4x4, a UVG Premia bodied Mercedes Sprinter ambulance and a Premia bodied Renault Master PTS unit at Uckfield Ambulance Station in 1999, all with different liveries.

Sussex Ambulance Service fleet maintenance van, a 1993/4 registered Renault, in Lewes circa 1999.

Bognor's new ambulance station was officially opened by Mr Patrick Herbert, Chairman of the Sussex Ambulance Service Trust, on April 17th 1999. A typically inelegant modern industrial style building, it was the first of the new ambulance stations built by the service. It had been in use since the later Part of 1998 and replaced the town's previous ambulance station built in 1966 on the same site.

Eastbourne ambulanceman Steve Isted, pictured here wearing his chain of office alongside a Toyota 4x4 Paramedic Response Unit, was elected Mayor of Crowborough in 1999.

Instructor Neil Monery (right) with driving course members outside Thakeham House, Southlands Hospital, Shoreham in August 1999. Sussex Ambulance Service had centralised its training facilities into this building in 1997.

Sussex Ambulance introduced the new all green ambulance uniform in October 1999. Staff nationally had had a say in its design, and the green trousers, shirt (or blouse), jumper and blouson jacket were intended to visually differentiate ambulance staff from police officers

Achievement of Master of Science Degree

The Sussex Ambulance Service's Emergency Planning Manager, Andrew Parr, has been awarded a Master of Science Degree in Emergency Planning and Disaster Management from Hertfordshire University. He is one of the first to be awarded the degree in its new format. Andrew began his course of study in 1997 and graduated at a ceremony at St. Albans Cathedral at the end of 1999.

Andrew has been with the ambulance service for 31 years working in operations, control and training. He is also a member of the Directing Staff Team for the Institute of Health and Care Development.

Commenting on his achievements Andrew said that his study had given him the opportunity to consider emergency planning and disaster management in a very wide context, basing much of his study on a range of both national and international disasters.

Andrew said "I am certain that the Sussex Ambulance Service will benefit in terms of preparedness to respond to a major incident from my having completed this course."

- The Masters Degree programme is run by the Civil Emergency Management Centre at Hertfordshire University, and attracts students from all over the world.
- Andrews's dissertation examined various aspects of "Training in Major Incident Management in the Ambulance Service" throughout the United Kingdom.
- Subjects relating to the direct management of a major incident were also included, as well as considering potential problems which may occur in the aftermath of civil unrest.
- A number of contributions from people with first-hand experience of disaster management were also included in the program.

Extract from Ambulance UK, June 2000.

Ban on paramedics lifting patients

Patients will be moved onto ambulance stretchers in the street in all weathers to protect paramedics' backs. Health and safety officials have banned paramedics from lifting patients into the back of ambulances unless they have no choice.

The ruling follows a report into the Sussex Ambulance Service, which condemned the number of back injuries suffered by staff. Union bosses fear the process will be undignified for patients.

Glen Seeley, a Unison representative based at Brighton Ambulance Station, said "We are expecting a lot of complaints from patients and relatives upset about being transferred onto a stretcher outside, possibly in rain or snow."

RISKY

For years, paramedics have carried patients outside in a chair, which they have lifted straight into the ambulance. They have then transferred them onto a stretcher.

The inspection, carried out by the Health and Safety Executive in November last year, found this practice to be against the rules about lifting, which were passed in 1992.

Instead, they want crews to stop in the street to shift patients onto stretchers, which can be easily loaded into the ambulance.

Trevor Jennings, health and safety risk manager for the service said "The use of the carry chair puts a terrible strain on backs." Mr Jennings said paramedics would have to make sure patients were "appropriately dressed" during the winter or cover them with blankets.

The practice has already been adopted in parts of Sussex. A memo to all staff outlining the changes will be sent but the service accepts that occasionally paramedics will have to lift patients.

Mr Seeley said the hills of Brighton and Hove could make the procedure well-nigh impossible without the help of another crew. He said "It will be extremely difficult for us to do this in some steep streets in Brighton. Patients are a high priority for paramedics but our number one priority has to be our own health."

From March 1999 to March 2000, 49 acute back injuries were reported by Sussex paramedics. To protect staff, Mr Seeley and other Unison representatives want the service to buy ambulances with ramps.

Mr Jennings and other ambulance bosses across the South-East are looking into prototype vehicles with ramps and tailgate lifts, which could gradually be brought into service.

Extract from the Argus, 14th March 2000.

The Sussex Police Air Support Unit, Hotel 900, at Shoreham Airport in May 2000. On the left is one of the new Jakab bodied Mercedes Sprinter ambulances, then a Honda paramedic motorcycle, a Vauxhall rapid response vehicle and a Toyota 4x4.

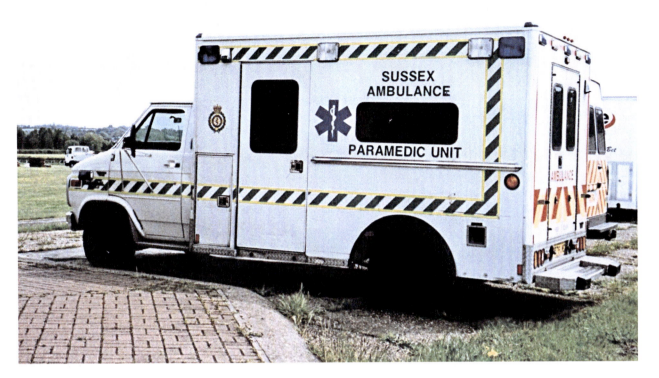

Sussex Ambulance Service Chevrolet ambulance at Plumpton Racecourse 24th May 2000.

Sussex Ambulance Service Paramedics undertaking the services first single responder driving course with three of the new fleet of Vauxhall Vectra response vehicles at Shoreham Ambulance Station circa June 2000.

Ambulance Care Assistants at Chichester Ambulance Station with a new 2000 registered Renault Master PTS unit. Both girls are wearing the pale green tops issued to second tier staff at this time, as opposed to the darker green tops worn by front line staff.

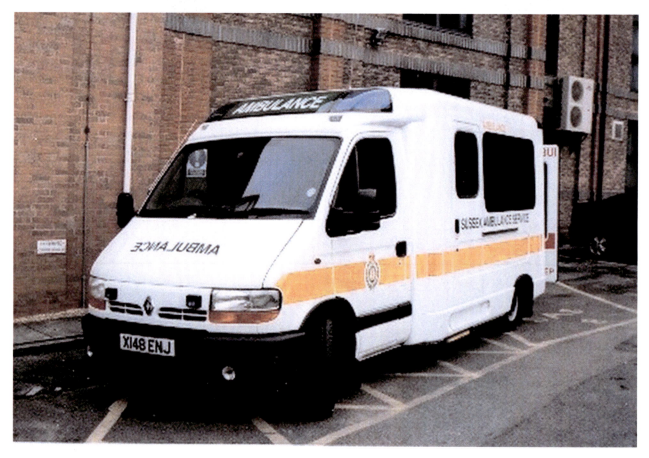

Distinguishable by its orange stripes, this UVG bodied Renault Master parked at the rear of SAST's Lewes headquarters in April 2001 is one of the new urgent care ambulances first trialled in the Adur district in February 2000 to deal with doctors urgent hospital admissions.

Sussex ambulance services may be merged with Kent

By Peter Homer

Ambulance services in Sussex could be merged with neighbouring Kent, under far-reaching new proposals unveiled by the NHS executive.

West Sussex used to have its own service, and then it joined with East Sussex to create a pan-Sussex ambulance trust, with a headquarters in Lewes.

If the new scheme goes ahead, it will involve a huge area, stretching from Chichester, in the west, right across to Sheerness, in the east.

A statement issued by the executive said that giving faster, more consistent and higher quality care to patients by reshaping the way ambulance services were delivered in the south east region lay at the heart of proposals now going to public consultation.

It said there were no plans to relocate or reduce the number of ambulance stations as part of the consultation, although individual ambulance trusts might be reviewing their estate as a separate exercise.

"Ministers have approved three months' public consultation on proposals to modernise ambulance services and provide a truly patient-centred service," it added.

A preferred option was to create three new ambulance trusts for the south east region, covering Buckinghamshire, Northamptonshire, Oxfordshire and Berkshire; Hampshire and Surrey; and Kent and Sussex.

A consultation document described how ambulance services must continue to develop if they were to make the maximum contribution to a modern NHS.

"Leaders of ambulance services in the region have been working together to create a joint vision of their role in the future," the statement added.

They wanted to see a service that delivered the best care for the individual patient's needs, gave consistent high-quality care based on evidence and best practice, made use of new technologies so that it could respond to patients' needs more quickly, ensured staff were well trained and motivated and had the skills they needed, and collaborated across organisations to give better support to staff and maximise the resources available for the care of patients.

The document set out how region-wide support services and functions – such as control and communications – would underpin the essential day-to-day delivery of ambulance services in local communities across the south east.

Certain other services would be organised at a sub-regional level, although on a wider scale than at present.

Particular emphasis was put on strong local identities. "People in the region require local, flexible and responsive ambulance services," the report added.

"These can only be provided by maintaining strong local identities and ensuring a close working relationship with other partners, including patients and carers."

Strong local relationships would require strong local operational ambulance divisions.

These were a key feature of how the three new trusts would be organised if the preferred option was approved by ministers after public consultation.

Cutting from the West Sussex Gazette, 10th May 2001.

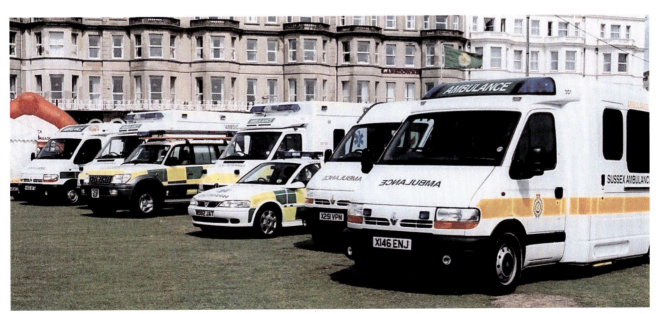

Vehicles on display at the 2001 Eastbourne 999 Show.

A brand new Jakab bodied Mercedes Sprinter at Lewes Ambulance Station in 2001.

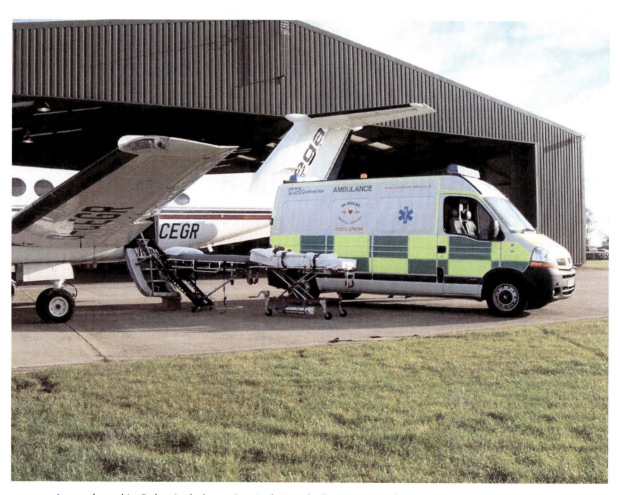

Lewes based In-Pulse Ambulance Service's Vauxhall Movano at the Cega Air Ambulance base on Goodwood Airfield circa 2001.

Presentation of Diamond Jubilee Medals to the staff at Bexhill
Ambulance Station by the Mayor of Bexhill in 2002.

SAST's Annual Award Ceremony held at the Barnsgate Manor Hotel, Herons Ghyll, in September 2002.

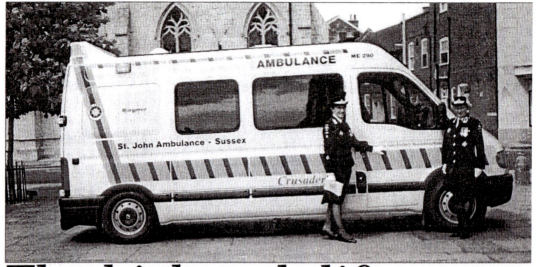

The high-tech life-saver

FIRST aiders in Sussex celebrated the dedication of their new ambulance last Sunday.

A £40,000 Crusader 900 has been bought by St John Ambulance, thanks to funds raised through Littlehampton-based county president Susan Cheney and her Nonacentenary Appeal.

More than 300 people attended Chichester Cathedral for an Evensong service, followed by the dedication by the Dean of Chichester, the Very Rev John Treadgold.

Mrs Cheney said: "The £40,000 ambulance has been the result of much hard work and many fund-raising events over the past two years and I would like to thank the many people and organisations who supported the appeal, for their generosity."

Among guests at the service were supporters and members of St John Ambulance.

Mrs Cheney said: "It gave us the chance to say thank you. So often people give to these things and never get a chance to see the end result.

"Here, they were able to look at it, the equipment and even get in it. It was a very good and happy day."

Three standards were paraded during the service, including the six to eight-year-old Badgers, the Cadets and the County Colours.

Guests included the Lord Lieutenant Hugh Wyatt, the High Sheriff Graham Fergu-

son, and their wives, other dignitaries and representatives, plus the chief president of St John Ambulance The Hon Lady Barttelot, who congratulated everyone on reaching the target.

Also represented were Arun Choral Society, Littlehampton Bonfire Society, Inner Wheel and many more groups and individuals.

Mrs Cheney presented the ambulance to county commissioner Rosslyn Stenning, on behalf of the county president's committee.

The high-tech Crusader will be based in Ringmer, centre of the county, which lost its ambulance and equipment in the floods at Lewes during the winter.

A further £10,000 raised said Mrs Cheney, would be split into sums of £500 for each division.

*Littlehampton St John Ambulance division will be taking delivery of a new vehicle in the autumn, thanks to fund-raising and a generous legacy.

The president's committee provided a further £100 enabling the group to keep its unique number plate which had originally been bequeathed to them — LSTA 999.

Mrs Cheney said old ambulances were taken to places such as Bosnia and Third World countries, where they were desperately needed.

Cutting from the Littlehampton Gazette 26th July 2001.

Brew time for PTS Staff at Brighton Ambulance Station, September 2001.

Sussex Ambulance Service Paramedic awarded MSc in Cardiology

Phil Lewis, a paramedic based at Burgess Hill, has been awarded the MSc in Cardiology from the University of Brighton.

Phil joined the Sussex Ambulance Service in 1992 and was initially based at Crawley Ambulance Station undertaking Patient Transport work. He became a trainee Ambulance Technician in 1994 and was upgraded to Technician in 1995, and in May 1997 Phil qualified as a Paramedic. In September 2000 he successfully obtained a place on the MSc Cardiology course. He was supported jointly by the SAST and the Ambulance Service Association through their Professional Awards system.

John Kirby, Director of Personnel for Sussex Ambulance Service said "The Trust is committed to supporting its staff and encourages staff development. We have supported one or two members of staff on this course during the past few years, and will continue to do so. Cardiology is a particularly useful expertise for practising paramedics and we regard cardiac care as a high priority. In addition, this is a post-graduate qualification which encourages students to undertake and apply their research for the benefit of patients in Sussex. We are delighted with Phil's achievement."

Phil is currently seconded to the Sussex Police Air Support Unit where he flies to incidents in the Police helicopter as a member of the Air Support Unit team.

Extract from Ambulance UK, February 2003.

Located on the Terminus Road trading estate to the south of Chichester railway station, the cities new ambulance station was officially opened by Patrick Herbert, Chairman of the Sussex Ambulance Service Trust, on June 21st 2003. This modern industrial style building replaced the city's old ambulance station in Summersdale Road.

LOTTERY BOOST FOR HEART PATIENTS

Thirty state-of-the-art defibrillators will soon be treating cardiac patients across the county after a lottery windfall. Ambulance bosses have been awarded £270,000 from the National Lottery to buy the vital equipment used by paramedics.

The services currently receives between 30 and 40 calls a day from patients suffering chest pains, many of which later turn out to be cardiac related. National research has proved that, in most cases, the earlier treatment is started with thrombolysis 'clot busting' drugs the better the outcome.

To do this, detailed information on the patient's condition is needed as soon as possible. The new 12 lead defibrillators cost £9000 each and as well as 'shocking' the heart, also enable paramedics and technicians to gain a print-out of vital information, at the patient's bedside or on the way to hospital. This crucial information will allow paramedics to administer clot-busting drugs straight away if necessary, gaining vital minutes of treatment. An added bonus is that the information can also be sent ahead electronically to the hospital, where it can be looked at and further treatment decided upon before the patient has even arrived.

Sussex Ambulance Service has 86 ambulances in total across the county and has recently purchased more than 40 of the new-style defibrillators itself. The successful bid to the National Lottery's New Opportunities Fund means the entire ambulance fleet can now be equipped with the latest cardiac care technology far more quickly than otherwise could have been managed.

Clive Butler, coronary care lead for Sussex Ambulance Service said, 'Being able to fully equip all our ambulances means that we can offer the same high level of cardiac care right across Sussex. Our staff will shortly be undergoing training both in the transmission of the information to the hospitals and in administering the necessary drugs, and as soon as this is completed, patients will be able to benefit immediately.'

Extract from the Gazette, 9th July 2003.

Paramedic course members at Thakeham House, Southlands Hospital, autumn 2003

L/R back row: Dave Bull, Rob McClew, Dave Croucher. Front row: Neil Harrison (instructor) Becky Sullivan, Emma Kemp, Katherine Peters and Jon Steel (instructor)

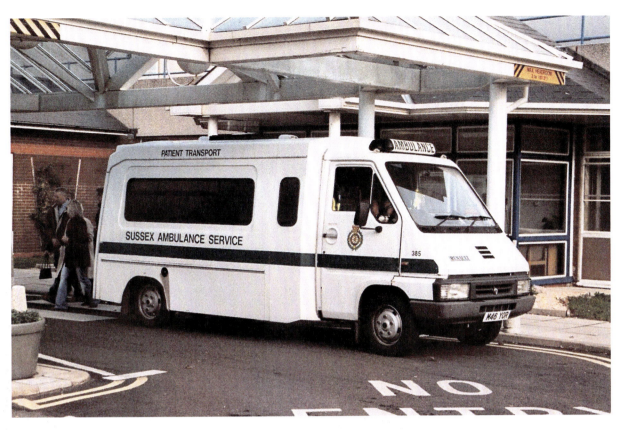

M46 YOR, a 1994/95 registered Renault Master PTS unit, fleet number 385,
at Eastbourne General Hospital in 2003.

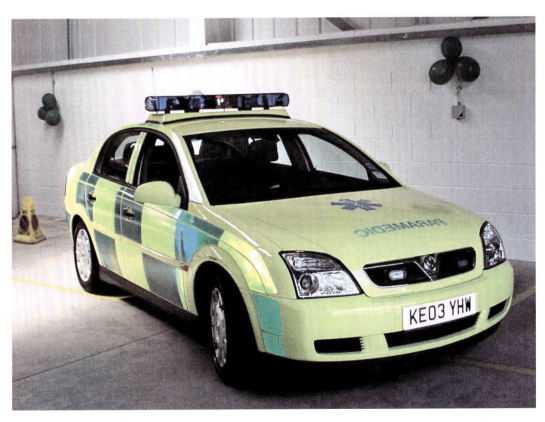

One of the new fleet of RRVs introduced to the county in 2003, this Vauxhall Vectra in the
garage at Chichester Ambulance Station is finished in the newly adopted all over yellow
European standard ambulance livery.

Two Hailsham based Mercedes Sprinter ambulances at Eastbourne General Hospital in 2003. V678 DYJ is an older 1999/2000 registered UVG Premia bodied unit, and RY52 BZL, aka 'Basil', is a 2002 registered Jakab bodied version.

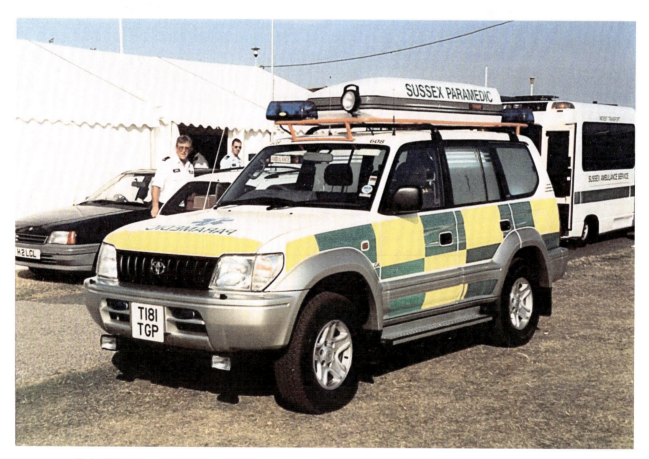

T181 TGP, a 1999 registered Toyota RRV, fleet number 608, at the 2003 Eastbourne 999 Show.

A 2002 registered Renault Master PTS unit outside the main entrance to Eastbourne General Hospital in 2003.

An O&H bodied Renault Master sitting case vehicle at Eastbourne General Hospital in 2003.

A Toyota 4x4 with two major incident trailers with the equipment they carry laid out in the rear yard at Chichester Ambulance Station in 2003.

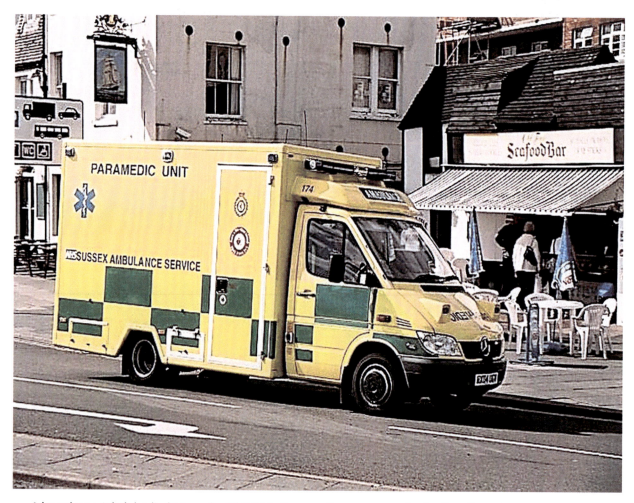

A brand new Jakab bodied Mercedes 416CDI in the new European standard yellow livery in Hastings in 2004.

Sussex Ambulance Service began operating motorcycle response units in 1996, initially operating out of Brighton Ambulance Station. Eventually there were motorcycles based across the whole of the county including Hastings, Eastbourne, Brighton, Worthing, Chichester, Burgess Hill, Horsham and Crawley. The standard motorcycle was the Honda ST1100 Pan European. This one was photographed at the Eastbourne 999 shows circa 2004.

Chichester Paramedic John Hopkins with members of the Selsey Community First Responder group at Chichester Ambulance Station in February 2004.

Burgess Hill Lions Club members presenting 'Trauma Teddies' to the staff at Burgess Hill Ambulance Station in 2004. This scene was repeated across Sussex as various other Lions Clubs gave these teddy bears to their local ambulance stations. They were to be given to young sick or injured children to comfort them while they were being treated in the ambulance.

The St. John Ambulance continued in its primary role as provider of first aid services at events both public and private. It was also part of the Sussex Ambulance Service's Emergency Reserve Scheme, and here Southwick St John Ambulance's 2004 registered Mercedes Sprinter RX54 WDU is on stand-by on Marine Parade, Brighton in 2004.

Pilots, Police Observers and Ambulance Paramedics, the flight crews of the Sussex Police
Air Support Helicopter Hotel 900 at Shoreham Airport in 2004.

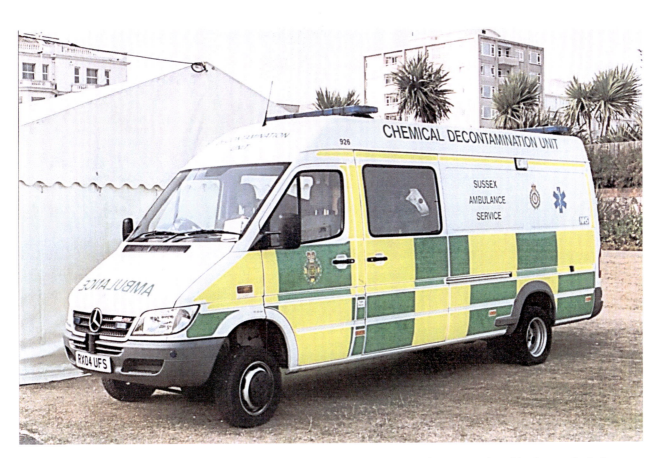

One of three new 4x4 CBRN Support Vehicles at the 2005 Eastbourne 999 Show, introduced by Sussex Ambulance
Service in 2004, they were based at Chichester, Brighton and Hastings, and carried an inflatable Airshelter,
decontamination, lighting and heating equipment.

SAST's Vehicle Maintenance Centre in Southdowns Road, Lewes, in 2005.

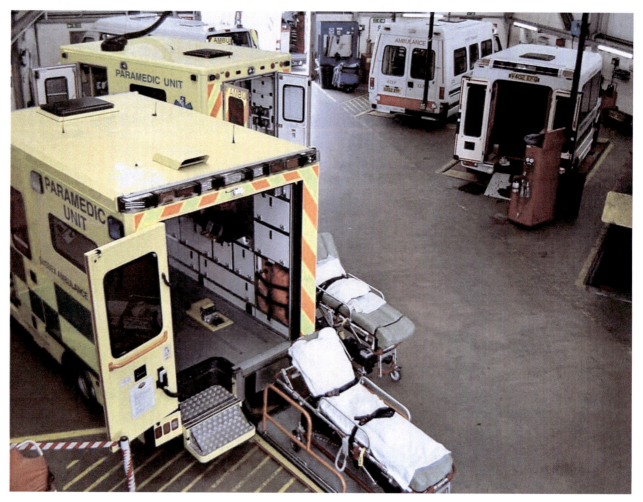

The interior of the Vehicle Maintenance Centre in 2005.

RX05 SWO, a Mercedes Vito Incident command Vehicle at the 2005 Eastbourne 999 show.

Goodwood Rescue at the start of the 2005 Brighton Speed Trials.

The independent Goodwood Marshals Club began operating a motorsport rescue unit in 1999.
In 2003 with the generous support of Volkswagen Commercials UK, this VW LT35 van was acquired and fitted internally as a rescue ambulance. It carried a full range of up-to-date medical equipment, including a defibrillator, and powered hydraulic cutting tools, commonly, known as 'the jaws of life', along with an extensive range of other rescue equipment. The unit was crewed by a Doctor or Paramedic plus a minimum of three motorsport marshals, trained and qualified in first aid and casualty extrication

South East Coast Ambulance NHS Trust

Sussex Ambulance Service merged with those of Kent and Surrey to form the South East Coast Ambulance Service NHS Trust on July 1st 2006. With its headquarters in the old Surrey Ambulance Service headquarters in The Horseshoe, Banstead, the Trust initially took over 63 ambulance stations, three emergency dispatch centres and various fleet support and training bases across the three counties.

Since 2006 many ambulance stations have been closed and their staff and vehicles relocated to more centralised Make Ready Centres or Hubs, the first of these in Sussex opening at Tangmere in August 2016, followed by a second at Polegate in October 2017. To maintain a local presence, small stand-by points known as Ambulance Community Response Posts were established in towns and villages across the county, where crews could take rest breaks or await calls during quieter periods.

Further new developments include the introduction of highly trained Hazard Area Response Teams; the first such was based in Kent and the second, Team West, at Gatwick, which became operational in 2012. These teams have the capability to operate in the most dangerous environments, including chemical and biological incidents, urban disaster and civil unrest situations. Specialist Paramedics with advanced training have been introduced to treat certain medical conditions and minor injuries at the patient's home address, avoiding the necessity of the patient having to go to hospital for treatment.

Many towns and villages started their own Community First Responder schemes, with volunteers trained by SECAmb staff and dispatched to incidents in their own locality by ambulance control. They are trained to initiate life-saving treatment and would be backed as soon as possible up by the nearest resource; i.e. an emergency ambulance or a fast response car.

In 2017 the service moved into a brand new headquarters building in Nexus House on the Manor Royal estate at Crawley. The building also housed the new Emergency Operations Centre for the Sussex and Surrey areas.

Undoubtedly many things have changed in the way ambulance services operate since their beginnings at the end of the 18th century. Better training, better equipment, better communications etc., but one essential thing that hasn't changed is the commitment of ambulance staff to deliver the best possible care to the communities they serve.

A SECAmb Mercedes ambulance at the Conquest Hospital, St. Leonards-on-Sea.